ENJOYING GOLF WITH NICK FALDO

ENJOYING GOLF WITH NICK FALDO

A personal guide to the game

with Mitchell Platts

St Michael

The publishers would like to thank the following
organizations and individuals for their kind
permission to reproduce the illustrations in this book:
All Sport 36 top left, 50, 58 top, 125 bottom, 178;
Associated Sports Photography 1, 14, 34, 53 bottom,
62 top, 99, 100 right, 102, 134, 149 right, 166 left,
169, 187; BBC Hulton Picture Library 40 top, 51 top,
122 left; Carroll and Company Limited 64 bottom, 79
bottom; Peter Dazeley 8 bottom, 9, 11 left, 13, 22
top, 28, 35 left, 43, 44, 45, 54, 55, 58 bottom, 59 left,
60, 77 top, 85, 86, 87, 95, 96-7, 106, 124 right, 132,
140 bottom right, 147, 149 left, 150, 155, 156, 159
bottom, 167, 168, 170, 171 bottom, 172, 173, 175,
177 bottom, 179 top, 182 left, 189; Mary Evans
Picture Library 40 bottom; Golf Photography
International 121 right; Dr L. A. Hardie 24, 36
bottom; Ian Joy 12, 49; Laurence Levy/Yours In
Sport 112, 145; Bert Neale 11 right, 32 top, 46, 47
left, 53 top and bottom inset, 59 right, 62 bottom
inset, 98, 100 left, 104 top, 121 left, 148; Popperfoto
47 right, 78 left; Tony Roberts 120; Royal St.
George's Golf Club 61; Phil Sheldon 2, 4-5, 6-7, 8
top, 10, 16, 18-19, 20, 21, 22 bottom, 23, 25, 26, 27,
29, 30, 31, 32 bottom, 33, 35 right, 36 top right, 38-9,
41, 42, 51 bottom, 52, 56, 57, 62 bottom, 63, 64 top,
65, 66, 67, 68, 70-1, 72, 73, 74, 75, 76, 77 bottom, 78
right, 79 top, 80, 81, 82, 83, 88, 89, 90, 91, 92, 93,
101, 103, 104 bottom, 105, 107, 108, 109, 110, 111,
113, 114, 115, 116, 117, 118-9, 122 right, 123, 124
left, 125 top, 126, 127, 128, 130-1, 133, 135, 136,
137, 138, 139, 140 top and bottom left, 141, 142, 143,
151, 152, 153, 157, 158, 159 top, 161, 162, 163, 164-
5, 166 right, 171 top, 174, 176, 177 top, 179 bottom,
180, 181, 182 right.

First published for Marks and Spencer in 1985
by Orbis Book Publishing Corporation Limited

This fully revised and updated edition published in
1986 by Orbis Book Publishing Corporation Limited

A BPCC plc company
Greater London House, Hampstead Road,
London NW1

© Orbis Book Publishing Corporation Limited 1985,
1986

Printed in Great Britain by McCorquodale Varnicoat,
Pershore

Mitchell Platts has travelled extensively to
all parts of the world in his position as golf
correspondent for *The Times*. He is a past
winner of the Association of Golf Writers
Championship and a member of
Ellesborough Golf Club in
Buckinghamshire, where he lives with his
wife, Hilary, and two children, Charlotte
and Elliott. He is also the author of *Nick
Faldo: The Rough with the Smooth*.

CONTENTS

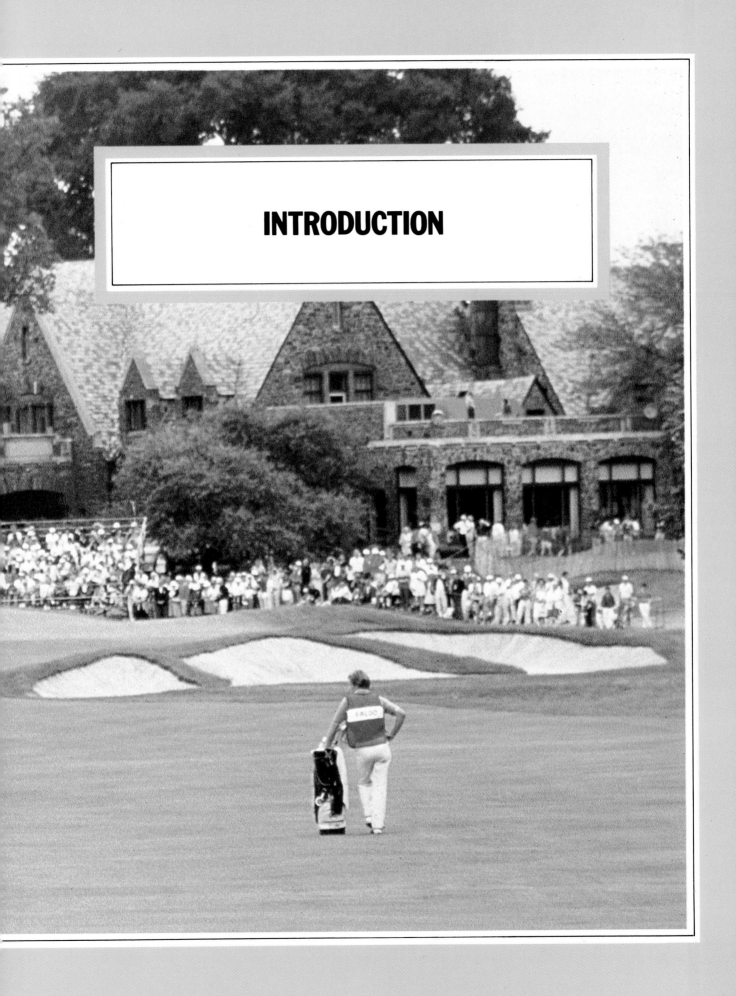

INTRODUCTION

INTRODUCTION

I fell head over heels in love with the game of golf during the Easter of 1971. The television was on in our house in Welwyn Garden City, Hertfordshire, and I watched, transfixed, as Jack Nicklaus challenged for the United States Masters at Augusta National. My courtship with golf began that moment and, fortunately for me, the relationship developed at a time when the game was enjoying a boom in popularity.

In Britain this upturn for golf had been triggered by the memorable achievements of Tony Jacklin. He had won the British Open Championship at Royal Lytham and St Annes in the summer of 1969, then the United States Open just eleven months later.

Tony was being hero-worshipped. There was an outcry for more courses to be built to cater for the thousands of newcomers who wanted to play. Suddenly the game with a hole in it had become more fashionable than any other. I joined the hordes racing to their local course. The Golf Rush was on and I wanted to be a part of it. Jacklin, whose father had been both a locomotive driver and a lorry driver, had hailed from humble beginnings. Now, in our terraced house, I dreamed of emulating 'TJ'.

Of course, at that time the country was bristling with youngsters who, instead of being captivated by soccer, were hoping one day to hit into the last green

Previous spread Nick Faldo goes for the pin at the 9th during the 1984 US Open at Winged Foot, New York.

Right Irresistibly drawn to golf at the age of 13, Nick Faldo is now established as one of the top names in British golf.

'When Tony won in 1969 I was in the grandstand next to the 18th green. He threw the ball high into the air in his moment of triumph and I was only a few feet away from catching it. I thought then how nice it would be to some day emulate Tony.'

Sandy Lyle on Tony Jacklin

Left A winning combination: at the Sea Pines Heritage Classic – which Nick Faldo won at Hilton Head, Ireland, in 1984 – Faldo works out his next stroke.

Above Tony Jacklin, at his peak during the late 1960s and early 1970s, was adored by every young aspiring golfer at that time.

the kind of controlled shot with which Jacklin had sealed his British Open victory.

Now they speak in terms of thousands falling by the wayside and the likes of Nick Faldo or Sandy Lyle or Sam Torrance being the fortunate ones to emerge and compete in a multi-million-pound arena alongside world stars like Seve Ballesteros and Tom Watson. But I believe that is a blinkered view. The game of golf, from its sketchy origins in the 15th century when 'golfe' was forbidden by an Act of the Scottish Parliament

Above Seve Ballesteros's consistent ability to get out of tight corners is the sign of a great player.

Left Sandy Lyle acknowledges the acclaim for his one-stroke lead after his final putt at the 1985 British Open at Royal St George's, Sandwich. Half an hour later, with all the final scores known, Lyle became the first British winner since Tony Jacklin in 1969.

Right You might get to play at Royal Lytham and St Annes but there's no guarantee of a police escort.

'Years ago I said I would jump off the top of the house when he won. I've changed my mind. There's too much celebrating to be done.'

Alex Lyle on his son's win at the 1985 British Open

under King James II, has evolved in such a manner that it can be enjoyed the world over.

For instance very few, if any, of you who read this book would ever have the chance of heading a goal at Wembley or hammering a six at Lords. In fact the best you can hope for is to be in the crowd watching a Robson or a Botham in action. But you need not be a professional to play the most famous golf courses in the world. You can pay a green fee and tee up from St Andrews to Pebble Beach. Moreover, how would you compete as an amateur defender against a surging Robson run or as an amateur cricketer bowling to a cavalier striker like Botham?

As an amateur golfer, however, you *can* compete against the professionals, because of the handicapping system, and, more importantly, two amateurs can provide each other with a fascinating challenge because their handicaps are regularly adjusted in order to equalize their ability and skills.

I was fortunate in that my game progressed, under the guidance of Ian Connelly – the professional at that time at Welwyn Garden City Golf Club – to such an extent that, within three years of purchasing my first set of clubs for £35, I was the toast of my club. I had collected nine amateur titles in 1975 including the historic English Amateur Championship which, like Jacklin's Open, I won at Royal Lytham and St Annes.

Where I was also fortunate was that the golf boom in Britain, initiated by Jacklin's transatlantic Open double, was being reinforced by commercial companies eager to join a sponsorship bandwagon. I respect the changing values of life, shaken and stirred by inflation, but the financial rewards of sport in general, and golf in particular, have risen to unprecedented amounts. When Tony Jacklin won the British Masters in 1967 it was worth

£1,218. When Seve Ballesteros won the Dunhill British Masters in 1986 the first prize was £33,333.

That, however, shrinks almost into insignificance when compared with the ever-increasing prize money of the Open Championship. In 1969, when Jacklin won, it was worth £4,250 to the champion. In 1976, the year in which I turned professional, it was worth £7,500 to Johnny Miller, the winner. In 1985, when Sandy Lyle won, he pocketed a cheque for no less than £65,000 and in 1986 Greg Norman took away £70,000.

The boom, of course, has not been restricted to Britain. In 1974 there was a total of 8.2 million dollars available on the American golf scene – today the figure exceeds 30 million. And the fairways of other circuits, like those in Australia and Japan, have become increasingly paved with gold.

I consider it my good fortune to have stumbled into this game, through watching by chance Nicklaus on television playing at Augusta, and to be benefiting now because of the rich harvest available. But I consider it my particularly good fortune to be a part of a game that allows man or woman, teenager or octogenarian, to express their love for life in an arena bequeathed by nature. And although the implements with which we play this game might be made by man, and they might have been revolutionized over the years, it is the land which has provided an open and healthy amphitheatre for more than 50 million golfers to enjoy themselves today.

Whether it takes you 66 shots or 106 to go round the course you can still enjoy the freedom of playing for four hours amidst the evergreens or everglades, in sight of sea or rolling hills, and recall that the challenge is no different now from when the game was first played at St Andrews.

If you don't believe me, and you have never played before, then I hope this book generates the desire to dash to the nearest golf club and book half a dozen lessons with the professional. That is the way I started and I have never regretted it!

Below Looking back over the burn to the 1st tee and 18th green at St Andrews, where golf has been played from at least the mid-16th century.

JOHNNY MILLER

The golden boy from California – he was born in San Francisco on 29 April 1947 – claimed stardom when he shot a closing 63 at Oakmont in 1973 to win the US Open. This astonishingly low score remains the lowest closing round in any major championship.

In 1974 he won the first three events on the US circuit and totalled eight wins that year to top America's money list with a then record 353,021 dollars. He became a phenomenon in 1975, winning the Phoenix event with a 24 under par score, and the Dean Martin Tucson Open (25 under par) back to back. His successes in the 1974 and 1975 seasons came to 13 tournament wins and more than 600,000 dollars in earnings. Miller was clearly riding the crest of a wave.

His form tapered off after his 1976 Open victory at Royal Birkdale, however, and he had to wait until the Lancôme Trophy in Paris in 1979 to triumph again. He has since taken his number of victories in America past the 20 mark and his career earnings to more than three million dollars. He first attracted attention in 1966 when he signed up to be a caddie in the US Open at the Olympic club, San Francisco, and qualified to play – finishing eighth!

Miller had started golf at the age of five and one of his first victories came in the US Juniors in 1964. He graduated from University in 1969 and, that spring, he earned the right to compete on the US Tour. It came as no surprise, as he had gained national notoriety at the Olympic Club (to which the US Open returns in 1987) and he was winning as early as 1971 when he captured the Southern Open.

There can be no doubt that when Miller is good he is very, very good, but when he is bad . . .! At his best, however, he is awesome to watch. He has power and precision off the tee, he can pepper the pins with the longest irons, and his putting touch can be so silky that he seems certain to hole every time, even when 30 feet from the hole. His victories off the American tour include the 1981 Million Dollar Challenge in South Africa.

Left Johnny Miller was a golf superstar in the 1970s and has earned in excess of 3 million dollars from the game.

JOHN MAHAFFEY

Three years ago John Drayton Mahaffey was born again. This, however, was not the result of some emotion-spinning revivalist meeting in America's Bible Belt. Mahaffey's re-entry into the human race came as he sat by the bedside of his dying father. It was then that his father spoke quietly to the son born in Kerrville, Texas, in May 1948. He pleaded with his boy to give up alcohol and to restore again the game that had brought them both so much pleasure throughout the 1970s.

It was a request Mahaffey could not ignore and, though his father did not live to witness the transformation, the Texan has done exactly what was asked of him. Instead of ending his days and nights staring into an empty bottle this psychology graduate went to work, grafting away once more on a golf game that had been good enough to win the 1978 US PGA title and make him one of the most formidable competitors on the hardest golf tour in the world. His reward came with his seventh win in the 1984 Bob Hope Classic, victory last year in the Texas Open and then the coveted TPC title in March 1986. In 1985 he finished ninth in the USA Money List, and pocketed $341,595 to take his career earnings to just under the magical 2 million dollar mark. 'What my dad said to me turned my life around. I was going backwards fast until that conversation. It was as though someone had turned the switch to get my brain working again,' he says. 'My only regret is that dad isn't here to enjoy the good times again with me. I just hope he knows what is going on . . .'

Below John Mahaffey made a big impact in 1986 by winning the tournament Players Championship at Ponte Vedra, Florida.

FALDO ON DRIVING

Let us get one thing straight from the start. I do not recommend that the average amateur, and certainly not the beginner, should even think of putting a driver in his bag – let alone wielding it on the golf course.

Now I'm not trying to be a killjoy. I know, when you watch the professionals power those drives towards the horizon, it makes you want to get on to the golf course and emulate them. But, take it from me, it is not the way to enjoy yourself.

The driver is a very difficult club to use. It has the least loft so for the average guy it can be a miracle even to get the ball airborne. What I suggest is that you don't look for miracles – you select a 2-wood or, even better, a 3-wood with which to drive. You will certainly obtain greater accuracy and the strange thing is that you will probably hit the ball consistently longer because of being able to strike the ball with what should become a familiar shape.

You see, some players prefer to shape the ball right to left, which is called a draw, and some play it left to right which is called a fade. The professional can almost certainly play the ball with both shapes, because there are occasions when it is required to bend the ball in the natural shape of the hole, but the majority have a preference for a draw or a fade.

In time the amateur will learn which shape naturally suits his or her game but, before driving into the wide blue yonder, you must first learn the fundamentals of golf. There are several golden rules to be followed, all of which you can learn by taking half a dozen lessons with your local professional, but first and foremost you must have a good grip.

Now I accept that to most people this is the boring part. The eternal excuse is: 'I feel quite comfortable the way I'm holding the club and I'm enjoying hitting the ball.' That, however, is a sure route to a golfing graveyard. You might, for a while, strike the ball with some certainty but, if you refuse to learn a good grip, then sooner rather than later you will find your limitations exposed. Quite honestly you do not see any good professionals with a bad grip. For if the grip is bad then the swing will eventually go haywire and there will be no other word for your golf but garbage.

The important aspect of the grip is not so much which type you choose, for there are several, but that the hands unite and that the palm of the right hand faces the target. If you were to pick up a tennis ball and throw it at a target and then stop as

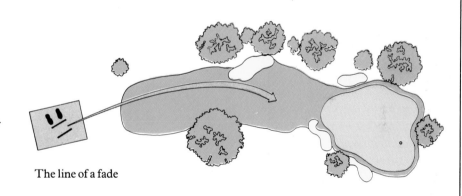

The line of a fade

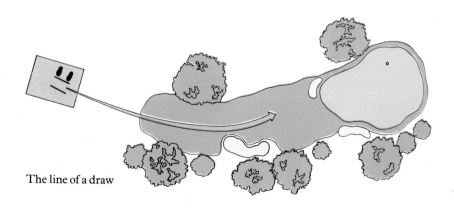

The line of a draw

the ball is released, you would realize that the palm of your hand is facing the target.

The classic grip is the Vardon grip, named after Harry Vardon, who won the Open Championship a record six times, and in this the little finger of the right hand rides over the forefinger of the left hand. The other familiar variation is the interlocking grip, favoured by Jack Nicklaus, which has the little finger of the right hand and the first finger of the left hand interlocked so as to increase the union of the hands.

Once you have obtained a good

Left Nick back in the groove again with his new swing during the Dunhill Cup at St Andrews (18th tee).

grip you can concentrate on other aspects such as the stance, where the feet, hips and shoulders must all be in a line pointing towards the target; the backswing, where the objective is to make a smooth shoulder turn so that the left shoulder touches the chin and the club goes back with natural acceleration; and the downward swing itself where the most difficult thing to learn is that you should first slide the legs laterally towards the target, which will automatically pull the arms down.

These are mere basics, and you will do well to listen and learn from your local professional, but they should lead to you being able to 'throw' the club away through the impact zone so that at the point of

impact, although the club is travelling at maximum speed, you are actually in the same position as you were when addressing the ball. Most important, of course, is that throughout this entire procedure you have kept your head still.

Now I am convinced that if you started out with a good grip but became too ambitious by using a driver you could soon become frustrated, which would allow bad habits to creep in. So I cannot stress too much that by driving with a 3-wood you will give yourself a more consistent start at each hole so that instead of repeatedly chipping out sideways from the trees you will, more often than not, be going for the green with that second shot.

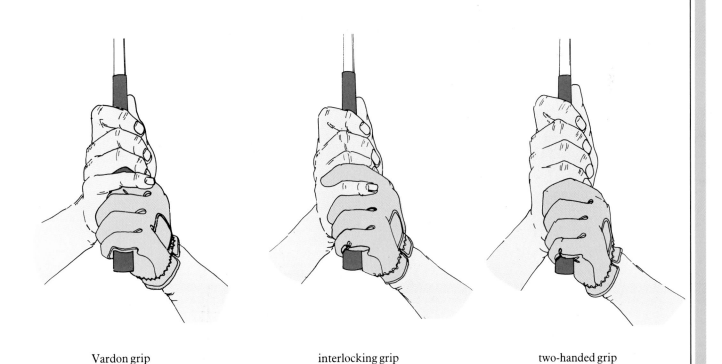

Vardon grip

interlocking grip

two-handed grip

CHAPTER ONE

A ROYAL AND ANCIENT GAME

CHAPTER ONE

A ROYAL AND ANCIENT GAME –

the first major tournament:
the British Open Championship

After decades of American domination in the British Open, the increasing strength of European golf was emphasized when Severiano Ballesteros scored his second victory, taking the title in 1984, then Sandy Lyle triumphed at Royal St George's in 1985. Moreover the Americans were shut out once more in 1986. Greg Norman, the Australian who had gained the reputation of being the finest golfer in the game today without a major championship to his name, strolled to victory by five strokes at Turnberry. He overwhelmed the opposition and the Turnberry course with the assistance of a brilliant second round of 63. In the past, question-marks had arisen over Norman's ability to cope with the mounting pressure of major championships but on the tough Ailsa course for the 115th Open he put that all behind him.

There was much criticism of the Royal and Ancient for the width of the fairways – 20 yards in places – though equally there was support for the governing body from some players and officials. The Royal and Ancient, however, will be concerned if apathy towards the Open Championship should spread. For the return to Muirfield in the summer of 1987 will remind people of the 1980 version when there was an exodus of Americans.

Even so there is now a greater challenge for them. The Americans, once the all-conquering heroes, the 'Goliaths' of the game, must return if only to repair their

Left Greg Norman follows Sandy Lyle on to the Open Championship roll of honour.

Previous spread Sandy Lyle nears glory at the 17th during the 1985 British Open at Royal St George's.

Right Jack Nicklaus arrived at Turnberry for the 1977 British Open as the reigning King of golf, but Watson took his crown.

'I partnered Jack in Hawaii in 1974. He had a lousy round but he was one under par for the day and he won because he managed his game and the course so well. He was conservative because he knew he had to be.'

Tom Watson on Jack Nicklaus

Below The 18th green at Turnberry.

injured pride. The European golfers, no longer the 'Davids' of the arena, are well aware that the last British player to win at Muirfield was Henry Cotton in 1948. That is the next blemish to be removed from the record books.

Time has decreed that golf, like any other sport, like any other part of life, should have its special eras which are usually characterized by a 'David' beating a 'Goliath': Liverpool being ousted by a Fourth Division side, or Steve Davis being out-potted by Joe Johnson.

But, occasionally, a 'David' rises to become a true world-beater, in sport a superstar, and so a new 'Goliath' is born only to become the latest prey of the hungry, unsung supporting cast. At Turnberry, in 1977, golf provided a classic example: a head-to-head duel between Jack Nicklaus and Tom Watson. It has been billed the greatest match in the history of golf – an excessive statement, perhaps, but every discussion requires a starting point and invariably it is the conflict at Turnberry which triggers a debate on this subject.

Consider the facts. Nicklaus had become the main man, the symbol of success – grind him into the ground and a player would be hailed a hero . . . or the new superstar. The trouble was that many had tried and failed. Nicklaus, from the moment he won the US Open in 1962, became the fat cat who sent the others scurrying like mice. Many played the game to put one over on Nicklaus but few succeeded. And, if they did, then glory was short-lived. Nicklaus was obsessed by wearing the crown. He had, quite simply, become a phenomenon . . . a winner, by that time, of five US Masters, three US Opens, four US PGA Championships and two British Opens.

Now a new 'gunslinger' had entered the golfing corral. Watson had already won a British Open, at Carnoustie in 1975, but far more important was his success earlier in 1977 in the US Masters. Watson carried the venomous label of 'choker' – a term applied to players who contrive to snatch defeat from the jaws of victory – but he had

TOM WATSON

Tom Watson's record in the British Open Championship is outstanding. The 'Huckleberry Finn' of golf – the Kansas-City born golfer (4 September 1949) got that tag because of his boyish looks and freckled face – first made his mark in the most prestigious championship in the world when he overcame Australia's Jack Newton by one stroke in an 18-holes play-off at Carnoustie in 1975. It was an important victory for Watson, because in America some observers had unkindly labelled him a 'choker', though he was to make them eat their words as the years unfolded. In Britain he became a hero as he meticulously collected five Open Championship wins, taking him to the threshold of equalling Harry Vardon's record of six Open triumphs. He captured the title for the second time in 1977, in that magnificent shoot-out with Jack Nicklaus, then won in 1980, 1982 and 1983.

Watson became the lord of the links and his ability to handle such courses was further emphasized when he won the 1982 US Open at Pebble Beach. That success will be best remembered for the brilliantly-executed pitch he holed from out of deep rough for a two at the short 17th. Nicklaus, back in the clubhouse, stared in disbelief at the pictures on television as his rival moved past him. And it was vintage Watson golf that took him to two

victories in the US Masters at Augusta in 1977 and 1981. In fact, from 1977 until the mid-1980s he was most certainly the dominant player in the world as he topped the American money charts four seasons in succession and then again in 1984. And on six occasions he has been named Player-of-the-Year in the United States.

Watson was a mere six years old when he was introduced to the game by his father, a scratch golfer, and he never looked back from the time he became a four-times winner of the Missouri State Amateur. He played for three years at Stanford University before graduating in 1971 with a degree in psychology. Watson is one of the most powerful strikers in the game, although he struggled through 1985 and the early part of 1986 trying to revitalize his game by overcoming putting problems.

Right Watson succeeds in getting out of a bunker during a US Masters tournament at Augusta.

CARD OF THE COURSE			
OUT			
HOLE	NAME	YARDS	PAR
1	Seal	362	4
2	Black Rock	391	4
3	Gyaws	381	4
4	Dunure	556	5
5	Greenan	210	3
6	Turnberry	577	5
7	Tel-el-Kebir	400	4
8	Postage Stamp	126	3
9	The Monk	419	4
		3422	36

IN			
HOLE	NAME	YARDS	PAR
10	Sandhills	437	4
11	The Railway	481	5
12	The Fox	432	4
13	Burmah	468	4
14	Alton	180	3
15	Crosbie	457	4
16	Well	542	5
17	Rabbit	223	3
18	Craigend	425	4
		3645	36
	TOTAL	7067	72

ROYAL TROON

Laid out on uncompromising linksland, the Old course provides a splendid challenge – particularly in windy conditions.

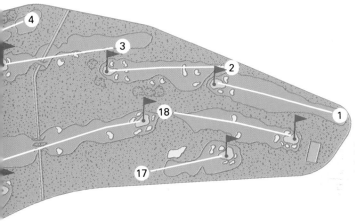

Below left The clubhouse at Royal Troon.

Below A famous golfing landmark – the 'postage stamp' 8th hole at Royal Troon.

JOSÉ-MARÍA CAÑIZARES

Like all the very best Spanish golfers, José-María Cañizares is a graduate of the Caddie School, the 'college' that either makes or breaks a youngster. In José's case it made him, forging a character and a temperament ideally suited to the pressure-cooker demands of top-level golf. This 39-year-old man is as quiet and unassuming off the golf course as he is on it. His swing is simple and relaxed, his attitude is as philosophical to bad luck as it is grateful when the damned ball pitches the right way for a change. Yet after turning professional in 1967, Cañizares had to serve a long and arduous apprenticeship before actually winning a tournament in Europe. That came in 1980 – after two play-off defeats by Nick Faldo – when he won the Jersey Open and the ill-fated Bob Hope Classic. In 1981 he took the Italian Open and in 1983 again won the Bob Hope title. In fact, throughout the 1980s he has been a model of consistency, picking up a decent pay cheque practically every week to reflect the accuracy and effectiveness of his play. In 1980 he was seventh on the Money List and since then has been 10th, 11th, fourth, eighth, eighth. It is a consistency that is often highlighted by spectacular scoring bursts, none more exciting than the tricks he pulled off during the 1978

Swiss Open, high in the Alps at Crans-sur-Sierre. He ended round two with five consecutive birdies and began round three with six on the run, followed by an eagle, to be out in 27 and match the world record for nine holes. To date he has won just under £400,000 in Europe and

despite greying hair and advancing years has the sort of game to double that amount at least before he retires to his place in the sun. Cañizares has also played in three consecutive Ryder Cups, including the historic 1985 victory, and in six World Cups.

Right José-María Cañizares has risen from the caddie ranks to be recognized as one of Spain's – and Europe's – outstanding golfers.

Left Nicklaus (left) and Watson take to the rocks as lightning strikes during the 1977 British Open at Turnberry.

Below Ben Crenshaw chased the leaders at Turnberry – but they set too hot a pace and he fell by the wayside.

silenced his critics. At Augusta, home of the US Masters, he beat Nicklaus – nailing the giant with a fast 20-foot putt for a birdie at the penultimate hole. Nicklaus, playing in the match ahead of Watson, had heard the roar which indicated a Watson birdie. He needed a three at the last . . . he took five. The crown had slipped, only a little, but it had slipped.

So to Turnberry. There was little outstanding to report from the first two rounds – save the coincidence that Nicklaus and Watson both opened with scores of 68 and 70. It meant that they would be paired together in the third round. The scene was set although nobody could have imagined, let alone predicted, the outcome of the next two days. Nicklaus and Watson were to exchange shots, just as

boxers trade punches, and to produce an epic encounter to glamorize Turnberry's baptism as a British Open venue.

Yet what was about to unfold on such hallowed turf might never have been possible. The battles that scarred the countryside as Robert the Bruce defended his castle (now ruined) at Turnberry were fought before the beginning of the evolution of golf. But the two great wars of the 20th century were responsible for pegging the progress of Turnberry. An airfield was established at Turnberry in the First World War, delaying the lengthening of the course from 13 holes to 18. But, between the wars, two complete 18 holes were built – the Ailsa, on which Nicklaus and Watson were now doing battle, and the Arran. The trouble was that in

the Second World War Mae Wests and flying boots once again replaced plus fours, and tarmac strips were laid where once springy green turf and sandy bunkers provided first-class golfing land.

It would have been a tragedy if such an exhilarating course had been lost for all time. But, under the guidance of a Scottish architect, Mackenzie Ross, a new Turnberry emerged six years after the war. The Ailsa course would have to wait a further 26 years before the Royal and Ancient of St Andrews, the governing body of the game and the organizers of the Open Championship, bestowed upon it the greatest honour in the game – that of staging the Open. But the wait was wholly worth while.

Nicklaus and Watson went out on that third day one stroke behind

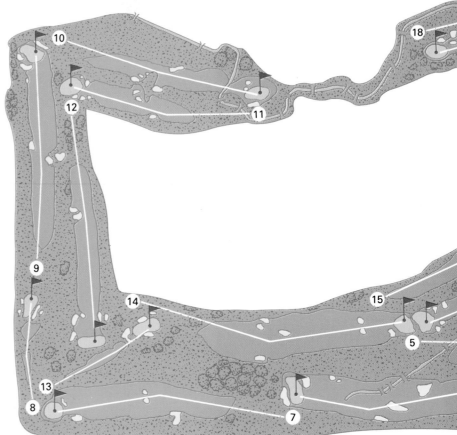

CARNOUSTIE

A tough, bleak, links course with frequent changes of direction, where the wind and the streams pose constant problems.

CARD OF THE COURSE			
OUT			
HOLE	**NAME**	**YARDS**	**PAR**
1	Cup	395	4
2	Gulley	432	4
3	Jockie's Burn	345	4
4	Hillocks	381	4
5	Brae	376	4
6	Long	529	5
7	Plantation	384	4
8	Short	169	3
9	Railway	425	4
		3436	36

IN			
HOLE	**NAME**	**YARDS**	**PAR**
10	South America	426	4
11	Dyke	370	4
12	Southward Ho!	476	5
13	Whins	161	3
14	Spectacles	482	5
15	Luckyslap	460	4
16	Barry Burn	248	3
17	Island	432	4
18	Home	440	4
		3495	36
	TOTAL	6931	72

Far left The clubhouse at Carnoustie.

Below Latin by name but not by nature – a bleak view of Carnoustie's 10th hole, called 'South America'.

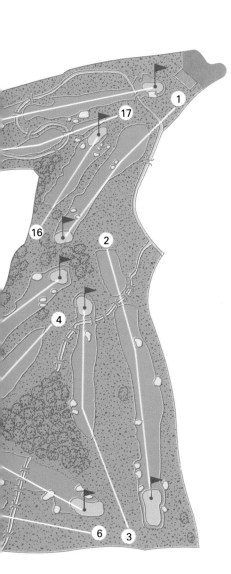

ARNOLD PALMER

If one man could be cited for starting the world-wide boom in golf then surely it would be Arnold Palmer. He started the explosion by taking the game into the American kitchens so that it became as popular with housewives as it already was with the true golfing aficionados. *Moreover, he transformed the British Open by pitching up for the 1960 Centenary Open at St Andrews, where he was edged out by Kel Nagle, then returning to win in 1961 and 1962. Palmer won the hearts of the British spectators with his approach to the game. He hitched up his trousers and went for broke. He drew the driver, drilled the ball, then smashed the next shot.*

Palmer became a great ambassador for the game with his swashbuckling, never-say-die approach, and his popularity has never waned. He has been honoured by many people from many nations during a distinguished career both as a player and a businessman. He was absolutely delighted in 1980 when Deane Beman, the US PGA Tour Commissioner of Golf, informed him that from 1981 the leading money winner on the circuit would receive the Arnold Palmer Award. In fact Palmer was the leading money winner himself in 1958, 1960, 1962 and 1963. He had first come to

prominence by winning the US Amateur Championship in 1954. The son of a professional, Palmer had dreams of 'doing a Bobby Jones' but he elected to turn professional – because he needed the money! – and so started one of the most illustrious careers in the game. He won the first of 61 tour events by taking the Canadian Open in 1955, though he also underlined his skills around the world by taking 19

foreign titles including the British PGA Championship, the Australian Open and the Spanish Open. Born in Latrobe, Pennsylvania, on 10 September 1929, it could be stated that his career at the very top was restricted to six years. Between 1958 and 1964 he captured his two British Opens, four US Masters and one US Open. But he remains a national hero and he is still winning on the US Seniors Tour.

Right Arnold Palmer, who transformed golf's popularity with his fearless approach to the game.

the overnight leader, Roger Maltbie. In a matter of holes they had overtaken him . . . by the end of the round they were still locked together and three shots clear of their nearest rival, Ben Crenshaw. It was cut-and-thrust stuff, all the way, as they each shot rounds of 65. The only interruption came when thunder and lightning forced a suspension of play for 30 minutes. Nicklaus and Watson sought sanctuary among the rocks – gazing out to sea to Ailsa Craig, a rocky islet ten miles out in the Firth of Clyde, and to the peaks of Arran.

So the last day dawned. A day of brilliant sunshine with such a light breeze that once again conditions were just right for attacking golf to be played. If the 1977 Open Championship had not been a sell-out at the start, it was now. A huge crowd followed Nicklaus, by now a man close to Scottish hearts following his success at St Andrews in 1970, and Watson, the pretender to the throne.

It might appear strange, to those familiar with the achievements of Nicklaus, that initially he was an unpopular figure. He was a perfectionist – not that that offended too many people – but, more damning, he was the man who had overthrown the people's champion of the 1960s: Arnold Palmer. For eight years Nicklaus's spectacular achievements were tainted by a peculiar public resentment – until St Andrews in 1970.

There, in a play-off against the luckless Doug Sanders, who missed

a putt of less than three feet in the final round which would have given him the title, Nicklaus removed his sweater at the last hole. He drove and landed on the green and, with victory assured following his second putt, he tossed his putter towards the sky. Jack Nicklaus was a human being after all, and the Scottish people gave him a reception second to none.

Now, as he strode down to the first hole at Turnberry with Watson walking alongside, so Nicklaus felt

Right Nicklaus (left) and Watson were paired for the last two rounds in a legendary encounter at Turnberry.

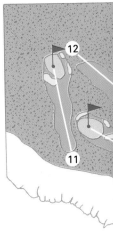

Above left Part of the dramatic setting at Turnberry with Ailsa Craig on the horizon.

Left The 12th hole at Turnberry, known as 'Monument' was lengthened for the 1986 British Open.

Above A typical view towards the green at the 10th – though the grass grew thicker in 1986 to plague contestants in the British Open.

TURNBERRY

The Ailsa is an exacting links course in a spectacular setting on Scotland's west coast, and the venue for the 1986 British Open.

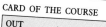

CARD OF THE COURSE								
OUT					**IN**			
HOLE	NAME	YARDS	PAR		HOLE	NAME	YARDS	PAR
1	Ailsa Craig	365	4		10	Dinna Fouter	460	4
2	Mak Siccar	440	4		11	Maidens	180	3
3	Blaw Wearie	475	4		12	Monument	395	4
4	Woe-be-Tide	170	3		13	Tickly Tap	385	4
5	Fin' me oot	490	5		14	Risk-an-Hope	440	4
6	Tappie Toorie	245	3		15	Ca Canny	220	3
7	Roon the Ben	520	5		16	Wee Burn	415	4
8	Goat Fell	440	4		17	Lang Whang	515	5
9	Bruce's Castle	475	4		18	Ailsa Hame	430	4
		3620	36				3440	35
						TOTAL	7060	71

PAUL WAY

There are many outstanding golfers, including Henry Cotton and Tony Jacklin, who have predicted that Paul Way will make the grade at the very top of his profession. The signs are that they might not be wrong about this young man, although illness and injury have contributed to his form disappearing for a time. He rocketed to fame by gaining a place in Europe's Ryder Cup team in 1983 – only his second full year as a professional – and partnering Severiano Ballesteros to gain 2 ½ points out of a possible four in the foursomes and fourballs. Then he went back out on to the PGA National course in Florida and beat Curtis Strange in the singles as Europe came within a whisker of overcoming the Americans on their own soil. He was a hero again in the 1985 match, in spite of the fact that some observers felt he should have been dropped because his performances had not been up to scratch, his strength being sapped by tonsillitis. Way, however, confounded his critics by linking with Ian Woosnam to beat Fuzzy Zoeller and Hubert Green in two fourballs encounters, then going on to beat Raymond Floyd by two holes in the singles.

Way, who also played in the 1981 Walker Cup, made his mark as an amateur by winning the English Stroke-play Championship that year. He turned professional later in 1981 and, in his first full season among the paid ranks, he won the KLM Dutch Open. He rose to 11th in the Order of Merit in 1983, dived to 26th the following season, but climbed back to tenth place in 1985 with the help of an extra-time win over Sandy Lyle in the Whyte and Mackay PGA Championship at Wentworth. He had given notice at the start of the year that he was ready for a good campaign by winning the South African Charity Classic. Way's idol is Gary Player, which is not surprising as he stands 5ft 8in and weighs in at 11 st. He has three sisters – 17-year-old twins Jackie and Nickie both have single figure handicaps.

Left Paul Way splashes his way out of trouble and goes for the pin.

'The wheel is turning. Jack (Nicklaus) and Tom (Watson) and Lee (Trevino) will come back and play some good golf but not as much. Hell, one day we're going to have to die and we don't want that to happen. But there is nothing we can do about it.'

Arnold Palmer in 1985 on the future of golf

Right Watson wins! Beating Nicklaus by one stroke, Watson's total of 268 set a new Open record by eight strokes.

again the might of that support. His opening drive missed the fairway but, as if lifted by the cries of the crowd, he still made a birdie. By the time he walked off the green at the short fourth, where he had made a two, Nicklaus was three ahead. It seemed, to all present at Turnberry and to the millions around the world watching on television, that this was to be no contest. Just a walk in the park for Nicklaus, and a humiliating drubbing for Watson.

Watson, however, sprang off the ropes. He birdied the fifth . . . the

seventh . . . and then the eighth. Nicklaus, visibly rattled, quite rightly called for the officials. He was worried about crowd control, with spectators encroaching on to fairways, and Watson agreed. Play stopped . . . and, as so often happens, the flair momentarily disappeared from Watson's game. He dropped a shot at the ninth and had to scramble for his pars at the next two holes. Then Nicklaus sank a 25-foot putt for a birdie so that he was two strokes ahead with six holes to play.

Watson halved his deficit with a

12-foot putt for a birdie at the 13th. Then, as he walked to the 14th tee, he took a hard swallow and said to Nicklaus: 'This is what it's all about . . . isn't it?' Nicklaus replied: 'That's right.'

It is hard to imagine that at that moment Nicklaus was thinking of anything other than victory. He had the experience, while Watson was still learning. And, more important, he had a one-stroke lead. What happened at the short 15th changed the entire complexion of the situation – Watson audaciously contrived to hole a putt

of fully 60 feet for the unlikeliest of birdie twos. He was level – then ahead with another birdie at the long 17th.

There was no sign of a choke at the last. Watson struck a killer blow – a searing 7-iron approach leaving the ball 18 inches from the hole. He would have two putts for the Open Championship from there because Nicklaus was 30 feet from the hole. Nicklaus, however, refused to go easy. He struck the putt with such authority that from

the moment the ball was sent on its way it had only one destination . . . the hole.

Watson, of course, still won. He holed his putt. And the two golfing gladiators walked arm in arm, both smiling, off the green. Nine years later in 1986, with the Open back at Turnberry and Sandy Lyle defending the Championship, Watson's winning last round of 65 to Nicklaus's 66 was recalled. For what also immortalized that performance was that it launched

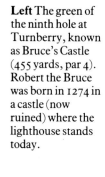

Left The green of the ninth hole at Turnberry, known as Bruce's Castle (455 yards, par 4). Robert the Bruce was born in 1274 in a castle (now ruined) where the lighthouse stands today.

Above Nicklaus sank his final putt of 30 feet at Turnberry but it still wasn't good enough to stop Watson.

Below The Arran Hills, over the Firth of Clyde, provide a spectacular back-drop to the testing Ailsa course at Turnberry.

MUIRFIELD

Swinging round the venue for the 1987 British Open

At Muirfield it comes down to how the Royal and Ancient, the organizers of the Open Championship, arrange for the course to be set up as the rough can be grown in, narrowing the fairways which are so well bunkered that there is always a premium on the drive. Your course management has to be at its best in terms of deciding whether to play short of the traps or to carry them with the drive. Then it is a question of judging the pitch and run shots into the greens, which is why the likes of Lee Trevino and Tony Jacklin, both masters at these shots, have played so well at Muirfield in the past. You must know the breaks on the greens so as to get the ball to run down to the pins because you do not want to leave yourself long putts.

Hole 1: *The key is usually the rough that the Royal and Ancient decide to grow. The fairway is extremely narrow – 20 yards or so – and the rough last time we were there was something like two feet high. So you don't want to miss the fairway. The second shot is a long iron into a green, which the land runs down to, so you can at least roll the ball down to it. There is quite a deep pot bunker back to the left which is to be avoided.*

Hole 2: *For this hole you turn 90° and go down the hill, with out of bounds on your left. A 3-wood off the tee is favourite, with bunkers to carry at about 235 yards. Then there*

is a pitch into a green guarded on the right by bunkers and on the left by thick grass. It is a birdie hole.

Hole 3: *Here you drive towards bunkers which are at about 280 yards, where the fairway narrows. It sounds a long way but in really dry conditions you could run the ball into them. So you might have to throttle back to a 3-wood or 1-iron. The second shot is a shortish one anyway so there is another chance of a birdie.*

Hole 4: *As the green is 40 yards deep it is possible to need to hit a 2-iron here, especially if it is cold and you are driving into the wind. The green, too, is a little uncharacteristic of a links green as the land falls right away at the back. It is a serious hole to miss as the approach is very narrow. A three is a good score.*

Hole 5: *This is a massive par five. The key off the tee is to miss the five bunkers down the right which are very much 'in play'. They start at about 200 yards and go through to about 290 yards so obviously they can all be dangerous at different times, depending on the wind. If you are driving downwind then you can get reasonably close to the green. But the second shot is equally dangerous as the green is heavily guarded by traps.*

Hole 6: *A dog-leg left with bunkers – four of them – down the left, which are not too bad. But it is the*

second shot which matters most, as you are obviously going in with a long iron and if you pull the ball severely then you can be caught out by the out of bounds, which edges its way towards the green. The penalty for going right of the green is a tough bunker shot for your third.

Hole 7: *Another tough par three. There are some massive, deep bunkers down the left side so they are very much to be avoided. The green is quite narrow and, once again, you can be hitting a lot of club into this one, depending on the direction of the wind. If the pin is put at the back then it could be as much as a 3-iron.*

Hole 8: *A hole with quite unbelievable bunkering down the right side, eight of the nine being virtually clustered together and 'in play'. The hole dog-legs left to right and it plays very long as the second shot is fractionally uphill. It is a very deceptive second shot as there are a couple of bunkers about 30 yards short of the green which automatically shorten everything in your mind. There is 'dead' ground over them so it is important to believe your yardage.*

Hole 9: *The famous ninth which has a very tricky bunker facing the drive. Together with the mound, it seems to cut into the fairway creating a very narrow strip. So you drive down the right and if you set yourself up there, then you can usually knock*

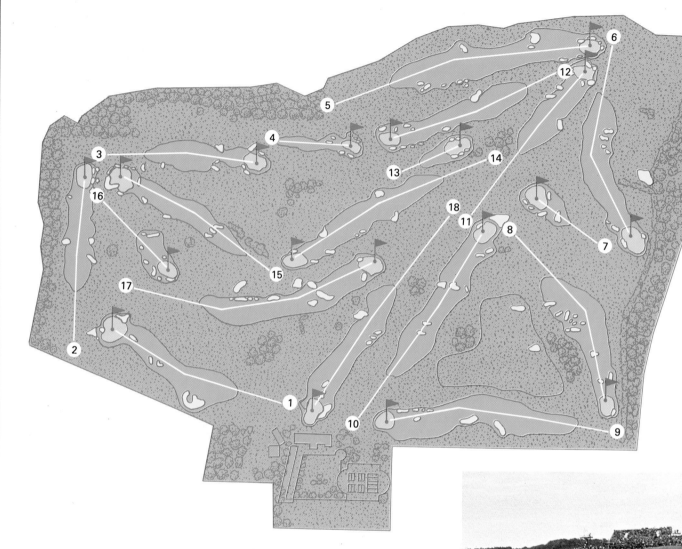

it on in two thereby missing the cluster of bunkers short and to the right. But if you leak the ball out then you will get caught out by the traps. Even so, you can land the ball short of the green and it will run up.

Hole 10: *This was a wicked hole for the last Open. The rough was very thick and, with the traps all strategically placed, it was a very difficult driving hole. There is a trap on the right at about 250 yards and*

another about 30 yards on, so you cannot try to carry the first because of the likelihood of running into the next. You must hit a precision drive down the left side, and then there is still a long second into a small green guarded by two bunkers on the right and one centre left. It is not too hard to drop a shot here.

Hole 11: *As you play over the mound, so this is a blind tee-shot. There is a trap out to the right and*

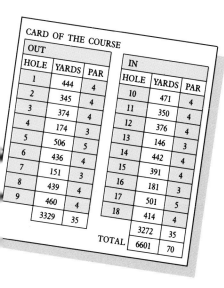

CARD OF THE COURSE		
OUT		
HOLE	YARDS	PAR
1	444	4
2	345	4
3	374	4
4	174	3
5	506	5
6	436	4
7	151	3
8	439	4
9	460	4
	3329	35

IN		
HOLE	YARDS	PAR
10	471	4
11	350	4
12	376	4
13	146	3
14	442	4
15	391	4
16	181	3
17	501	5
18	414	4
	3272	35
TOTAL	6601	70

Below Lee Trevino and Ken Brown assess their putts at the 12th during the 1980 Open at Muirfield.

the hole, if it is played into the wind, can be quite tricky because of the second shot. The green is completely circled by bunkers so the pin can always be placed in such a manner that any of the bunkers can be brought into play.

Hole 12: *A very exposed hole played from an elevated tee. Once again, there is a trap at about 250 yards, this time down the left, which comes into play. It is quite a difficult hole because the way you line up means that you must fade your shot left to right to avoid the fairway trap. It needs a good second shot, run into a green with a cluster of bunkers to the right which will catch a leaked approach.*

Hole 13: *A short, but teasing, par three which has a long, narrow green. It requires a precise, knocked-down shot, often played into an easterly wind. As the green is almost 50 yards long it is important to select the right club to reach the correct sector of the putting surface.*

Hole 14: *Three bunkers down the left, the first at about 220 yards, and one on the right narrow the driving area. The second shot goes downhill and as the hole is again very much exposed, the wind, usually left to right, makes it fairly hard to control the ball and hit a difficult green. The thing about Muirfield is that the bunkers are always in the right places . . . or the wrong places, depending on which way you look at it!*

Hole 15: *The fairway narrows considerably at around the driving landing area so, while you can go for*

a big hit, the name of the game could be to take a 1-iron or 3-wood. This is especially the case if the hole is played downwind, which would leave a second shot to be run in to the green. It is a tricky shot to play because the ground slopes off quite considerably and you have to judge it well to get the ball to run down the right of the green where most of the pin positions go. The cross-winds can also make it a teasing and tormenting shot.

Hole 16: *You usually turn back into the wind here so it can play up to about 200 yards, which means that a very good long iron shot is the recipe for the day. It is a very generous green but it is surrounded by pot bunkers so the tee-shot must be precise.*

Hole 17: *The bunkers down the left side off the tee are all in play and out of sight, so you are firing a driver almost into the horizon. The traps on the left are very severe and if you finish in one of them, then it calls for a sand wedge out sideways. It takes two massive hits in the dry to get there but generally a driver and a 3-wood will still leave you a pitch. The bunker guarding the front left of the green is very, very deep with a massive lip. The hole is a slight dog-leg version of the 14th at St Andrews.*

Hole 18: *A tough finishing hole. The drive must be aimed at the bunkers at about 255 yards up the left but cut away from them to find a fairly narrow hitting zone. The hole plays every inch of its yardage and there are some severe positions for the pin on the greens.*

Watson *en route* to the possibility of overhauling the record of six Open Championship victories established much earlier in the century by Harry Vardon. Watson, of course, missed his chance at Turnberry but he will endeavour to equal that record when he returns to Muirfield in 1987.

In essence Vardon was the first 'Goliath' of the game. The sport, or rather the Open Championship which was the first official professional showpiece, was dominated initially by Willie Park, Tom Morris Snr and Tom Morris Jnr. It was on 17 October 1860 that the first round of the inaugural Open Championship was played at Prestwick. A handsome silver-mounted red leather belt, worth £30, was the prize and there were eight contestants. The championship was played over three rounds which meant 36 holes in all as Prestwick had only 12 holes at that time.

Park won, as he did again in 1863 and 1866, but Tom Morris Snr claimed four victories: in 1861, 1862, 1864 and 1867. Old Tom, however, was compelled to give way to Young Tom, born in 1851,

as his son won three times in succession from 1868. The Belt became Tom Morris Jnr's property and the Championship remained in abeyance for one year until a new trophy, a Cup, was produced for 1872 on the understanding that it could never be won outright. Young Tom won again that year, and Willie Park also managed a fourth win in 1875, but although Jamie Anderson and Bob Ferguson both completed 19th-century hat tricks, it was Vardon who emerged as the game's first influential figure.

Vardon, first a pageboy, then a manservant and next an under-

gardener in the Channel Island of Jersey where he was born, turned professional at the age of 20. He was self-taught, with less than 20 rounds behind him, and yet he transformed the game. Golf, with its roots in Scotland, had mostly been played on the linksland close to the sea where raw, biting winds compelled players to take a wide stance and hit their shots as low as possible. Vardon, however, arrived on the scene with a narrow stance and an upright swing so that he was the innovator of the high shot. He imparted back spin on the ball and obtained the kind of precision that

Above Harry Vardon (at play) is the only man who has won the British Open six times. He is pictured here at Tavistock in 1921 with Ted Ray.

Left Three giant names in the early years of the British Open are those of Willie Park (wearing light suit, left), Tom Morris Jnr (wearing light trousers, centre) and Tom Morris Snr (at play). The photograph was taken at Leith links in May 1867.

IAN WOOSNAM

'Woosie', at 5ft 4½in, is the smallest player on the tour. But his lack of inches is more than compensated for by an abundance of Welsh spirit. He typifies the 'Bulldog Breed' of his compatriots Dai Rees and Brian Huggett with an aggression which often produces quite spectacular golf. Woosnam leapt into the limelight in 1982 with victory in the Swiss Open and has since become one of the most consistent performers on the circuit, pocketing a title every year. He has made two Ryder Cup appearances, forming a formidable partnership with Paul Way in the historic triumph at The Belfry.

Ian packs a mighty punch and is considered the tour's biggest hitter, with an average drive of 264 yards in 1985. That power, allied to a street fighter's instinct, helped him to his most satisfying success to date in the 1982 Silk Cut Masters, where he beat the likes of Seve Ballesteros, Sandy Lyle, Greg Norman and Nick Faldo in his native Wales. He nurtured his golfing muscle on the family farm and learned his golf at Llanymynech (which has 15 holes in Wales and three in England!). Although born in Shropshire he is adamantly Welsh, declaring: 'Both my parents were born in the principality and I'm a Taff to the core.'

Woosnam took the Scandinavian Enterprises Open in 1984 and, although he failed to register a European victory the following season, kept up his remarkable run by collecting the Zambian Open. Even so, 1985 in Europe was a memorable one for Ian. In addition to the Ryder Cup, he shot his career-best score in the Benson and Hedges, equalling the world record of eight successive birdies in a 62 to finish runner-up to Sandy Lyle, before helping Wales eliminate favourites Spain from the Dunhill Cup at St Andrews.

Below Ian Woosnam during the 1982 Benson and Hedges International at Fulford when he finished joint second. In the 1985 version he set a new course record of 62. He finished second then, though he will still rate more highly his joint third place in the 1986 Open.

Above The 18th green at Muirfield and the clubhouse which serves as the headquarters of the Honourable Company of Edinburgh Golfers, whose origins go back to 1744.

before had been considered impossible. Other golfers, by now, were using the overlapping grip, in which both hands are linked, but he popularized it to such an extent that it became known as the 'Vardon Grip'. Thus he became a cult figure and a player who, decade after decade, would stand comparison with each and every newcomer who strove to attain similar heights.

What is more, with the game becoming increasingly popular, Vardon became the first 'David' to cut down a 'Goliath' – the much respected John Henry Taylor –

thereby emerging as a superstar in his own right. Often imitated, but rarely equalled, Vardon became a giant so that the first true era of dominance by one player was born.

J. H. Taylor had won the Open – which by now was attracting an entry of almost 100 and being moved around the country – at Sandwich in 1894 and at St Andrews the following year. Vardon, however, beat Taylor in a play-off at Muirfield the year after that. In truth three players shared the glory as golf moved into the 20th century as James Braid, a joiner by trade, won the Open in 1901, 1905, 1906, 1908 and 1910 and Taylor, too, took his number of victories to five by succeeding in 1900, 1909 and 1913. Together, Braid, Taylor and Vardon were

referred to as the great Triumvirate but history dictates that in any era there is one star brighter than the others and that star was Vardon. Almost certainly his record of six Open wins would have been greater but for the fact that, sadly, he suffered from tuberculosis and that, following his sixth win in 1914, the First World War intervened.

When the Open resumed, at Deal in 1920, it was shortly never to be the same. George Duncan won that year and Jock Hutchison the next, but in 1922 the Championship was won by an American for the first time. Walter Hagen, a flamboyant character with an extravagant life style, silenced the British brigade. Indeed the 1920s were dominated by two

SANDY LYLE

As he fluffed his chip beside the 18th green at Royal St George's on 21 July 1985, so every 'ringside' spectator and armchair viewer cupped their hands over their eyes in dismay. Thirty minutes later Lyle, and his millions of fans, breathed a sigh of relief. He had followed Tony Jacklin into the record book by winning the Open Championship. It was a victory born in Shropshire where, at the age of three and wearing wellington boots, Lyle struck his first shot some 70 yards down the fairway. Lyle, coached throughout his career by his father Alex, the former professional of Hawkstone Park, moved through a fine amateur career, including Walker Cup honours, before turning professional in 1977. He soon underlined his rich potential among the paid ranks by topping the PGA Qualifying School tournament, then capturing the Nigerian Open in 1978. In 1979 he won the Jersey Open, Scandinavian Open and European Open on his way to becoming number one that season in the Order of Merit, and he held his place at the top the following season. He also made his name that season by winning the individual trophy in the World Cup.

There was no doubt whatsoever that Lyle was making significant progress, but it was not until late in the 1984 season that he galvanized his game to such an extent that he felt ready for the challenge of the Open Championship. He moved past Severiano Ballesteros to win the Lancôme Trophy in Paris, a particularly impressive performance, then streaked away with the Kapalua International in Maui, Hawaii, and put the icing on the cake by winning the World Open in Japan. Everything was coming up roses for Sandy, though there was a rather gigantic hiccup in 1985 when he tore up his card while heading for a score in the 90s in the Carrolls Irish Open first round. But one month later the resolute Scot was Open champion. He has been a Ryder Cup regular since 1979 and in 1986 he achieved another major breakthrough by winning the Greater Greensboro Open on the US PGA Tour.

Right Sandy Lyle, a cool, candid player whose effortless yet immensely powerful swing catapulted him to glory at Royal St George's in 1985 as the first British winner of the Open Championship since Jacklin.

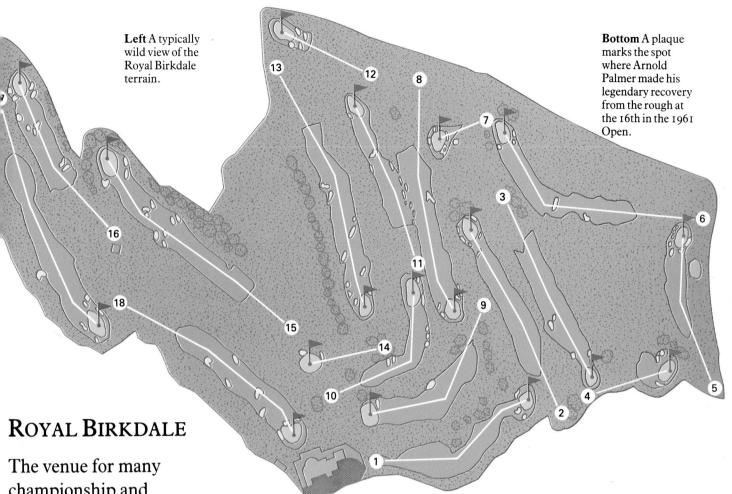

Left A typically wild view of the Royal Birkdale terrain.

Bottom A plaque marks the spot where Arnold Palmer made his legendary recovery from the rough at the 16th in the 1961 Open.

ROYAL BIRKDALE

The venue for many championship and international matches amid the sandhills of Lancashire's coast, where power takes second place to accuracy.

CARD OF THE COURSE		
OUT		
HOLE	YARDS	PAR
1	450	4
2	423	4
3	410	4
4	206	3
5	343	4
6	468	4
7	150	3
8	470	4
9	410	4
	3330	34

IN		
HOLE	YARDS	PAR
10	384	4
11	411	4
12	184	3
13	505	5
14	198	3
15	542	5
16	415	4
17	526	5
18	473	4
	3638	37
TOTAL	6968	71

Americans. Hagen captured the title in 1924, 1928 and 1929 and R. T. Jones, the legendary Bobby Jones, won in 1926, 1927 and 1930.

In truth the British people did not take too kindly to this American invasion. Nor did the Americans initially invite admiration of their deeds. Jones, for instance, tore up his card at the short 11th when competing for the first time at St Andrews in 1921. Quite simply, this was because he was so demoralized by the demands of the Old course. It was a rash act and one that he was later to regret. He worried for years over his stupid behaviour there – not surprisingly as the Scots regard St Andrews, the home of golf, as holier than the Catholics regard the Vatican. For it was at St Andrews that, on 14 May 1754, 22 noblemen and gentlemen subscribed for a silver cup, to be played for annually, and thus founded the Royal and Ancient.

Jones, however, was too astute not to learn from that incident. He not only became the most outstanding exponent of the game, of his time, but also – according to most of those who saw him play – a golfer whose ability and achievements would never be

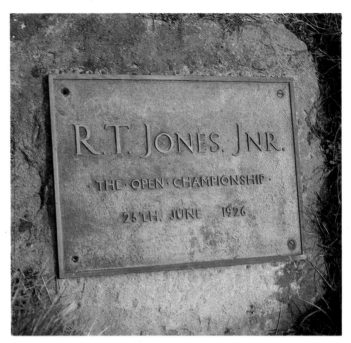

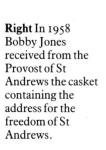

Right In 1958 Bobby Jones received from the Provost of St Andrews the casket containing the address for the freedom of St Andrews.

Below, centre The silver claret jug, awarded to the winner of the Open Championship, became in 1985 for one year the property of Sandy Lyle whose name was engraved alongside those of the greats of golf.

Left The plaque at Royal Lytham and St Annes which commemorates Bobby Jones's astonishing recovery in the British Open in 1926 with a shot of 170 yards from a bunker to the green at the 17th.

equalled. What is more, by the time in 1930 that he won the Open at Hoylake and the Amateur, as fate would have it at St Andrews, to complete a golfing Grand Slam (he had won the Amateur and Open titles in the United States), he was loved and respected throughout Britain.

Jones had earned this respect, in terms of pure golf, by winning his first Open Championship in 1926 at Royal Lytham and St Annes. There, in the final round, he executed a shot at the 17th which became part of the folklore of golf. Jones had attempted to shorten the dog-leg of a hole extending 453 yards but he succeeded only in putting the ball in a bunker. Al Watrous, a fellow-American with whom he was level in the lead at the time, had safely despatched his second shot to the heart of the green. Jones, facing an awesome shot of some 170 yards from out of the sand, struck the ball so cleanly with a mashie – equivalent in today's terms to a 5-iron – that it travelled over all the hillocks and scrub and on to the green. The shock to Watrous's system was too much. He three-putted . . . and the title went to Jones. A plaque which reads 'R. T. JONES JNR – The Open Championship, 25th June 1926' was erected close to the bunker to commemorate his stroke of genius.

In 1930, after his Grand Slam, Jones retired . . . by then a much loved man. His magnetism was demonstrated in 1936 when, on his way to the Olympic Games in Berlin that year, he could not resist the temptation of stopping off in Britain to go to St Andrews. When he teed off there was hardly a soul to be seen, but within minutes the news of his presence had spread throughout the 'auld grey toon' and more than 2,000 people turned out. He returned again, in 1958, as the non-playing captain of the American Eisenhower team and to be given the Freedom of the City. Jones explained to the gathering that the more he studied the Old course of St Andrews the more he loved it. Then their adopted son movingly said: 'I could take out of my life everything except my experiences at St Andrews and I'd still have a rich, full life.'

Hagen, however, was a contrasting figure. He did not have the tee-to-green brilliance of Jones for as Tommy Armour, who was to win the 1931 Open at Carnoustie, said: 'It is nonsense to talk about who was the greatest golfer in the world. All you can say is that there have been none greater than Bobby Jones.' But Gene Sarazen, who followed Armour as the tenth American winner of the Open in eleven years, said of Hagen: 'Whenever a tournament professional stretches a fat winning cheque between his fingers, he should give silent thanks to Hagen.'

Quite simply Hagen roared in the 1920s. He crossed swords with officials. He argued that golfers were not second-class citizens and that they should be allowed in clubhouses. When he was refused entry he parked his car, usually a chauffeur-driven limousine, close to the clubhouse and from the boot the butler would serve champagne and oysters. Hagen – nicknamed 'The Haig' – played in silk shirts with monograms and two-tone shoes. He wore hand-made suits and solid gold cuff links. He

'Whenever I fail to stop Jones the rest of you (his fellow professionals) curl up and die too. All the goddam amateur has to do is show on the first tee, and the best pros in the world throw in the towel. What are we going to do about it?'

Walter Hagen on Bobby Jones

Left Walter Hagen, four-times winner of the British Open title, is seen here at Sandwich nearing victory in 1928.

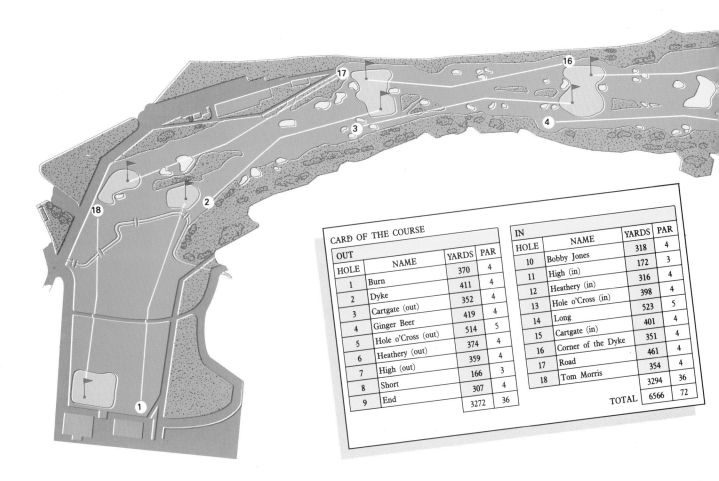

CARD OF THE COURSE			
OUT			
HOLE	NAME	YARDS	PAR
1	Burn	370	4
2	Dyke	411	4
3	Cartgate (out)	352	4
4	Ginger Beer	419	4
5	Hole o'Cross (out)	514	5
6	Heathery (out)	374	4
7	High (out)	359	4
8	Short	166	3
9	End	307	4
		3272	36

IN			
HOLE	NAME	YARDS	PAR
10	Bobby Jones	318	4
11	High (in)	172	3
12	Heathery (in)	316	4
13	Hole o'Cross (in)	398	4
14	Long	523	5
15	Cartgate (in)	401	4
16	Corner of the Dyke	351	4
17	Road	461	4
18	Tom Morris	354	4
		3294	36
	TOTAL	6566	72

Right The first green (left foreground) at St Andrews.

48

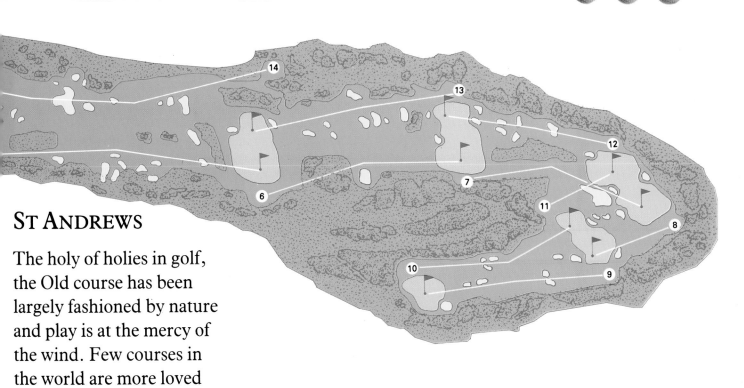

St Andrews

The holy of holies in golf, the Old course has been largely fashioned by nature and play is at the mercy of the wind. Few courses in the world are more loved or respected.

Left The view over the Swilcan Burn to the 18th green at St Andrews. The grey building on the left is the headquarters of the Royal and Ancient Golf Club which was founded in 1754.

49

GARY PLAYER

Gary Player must be the greatest globetrotting golfer the world has ever known. In spite of having to commute from Johannesburg, South Africa – where he was born on 1 November 1935 – he has won more than 130 tournaments around the world. His latest successes have come on the US PGA Seniors Tour – though it all began for Gary back in 1956 when he won the first of his 13 South African Opens. He then set off on his travels, although soon after arriving in Britain he was advised by a fellow professional, with whom he was staying in bed-and-breakfast stops around the tour, that he would be best advised to go home because he did not have a good enough swing to make a financial success of the game.

There is no more determined golfer in the history of the game than Player, however. He was soon winning around the world – the 1957 Australian PGA title and the 1958 Kentucky Derby Open were among his early successes – but it was the British Open which provided the real launching pad to an amazing career when he won at Muirfield in 1959. He was to go on and win tournaments in four different decades. He scored his 19th, 20th and 21st victories on the US Tour with an astonishing hat-trick in 1978 in the US Masters, Tournament of Champions and Houston Open. It was his third US Masters triumph. He had also won three British Opens – the other two came at Carnoustie in 1968 and at Royal Lytham in 1974 – and he has twice taken the US PGA Championship as well as the US Open in 1965. At the age of 48 he shot a tournament record nine below par 63 in the second round of the 1984 US PGA Championship at Shoal Creek – finishing joint second behind the equally evergreen Lee Trevino. He was one of the original inductees into the World Golf Hall of Fame at Pinehurst.

Left Following Locke's successes in the Open in the 1950s Gary Player kept South Africa to the fore by winning the title for the first time in 1959.

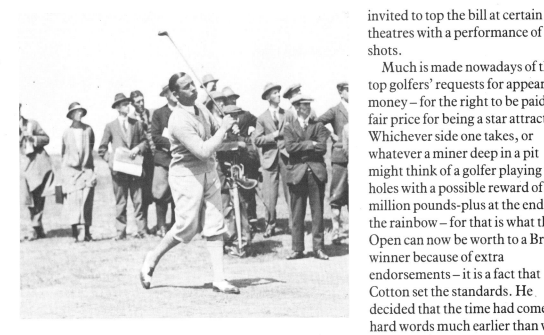

Right Hagen the winner by a stroke – that was the result when Walter Hagen won his first Open Championship at Hoylake with a score of 301 for four rounds.

treated bills like confetti, showering dollars in restaurants and hotels around the world, so that life was one, swinging party – on and off the fairways. And he coined the classic remark: 'So many people today never have time to stop off and smell the flowers as they go through life.'

In Britain it was the seed that sowed a new era. It was time – at least, Henry Cotton thought it was time – both for the American dominance to be ended and for a British player to take his deserved reward from a game which was now so popular that admission to the Open Championship was charged. Cotton almost hero-worshipped Hagen; he travelled to America in 1928 and watched, in stunned amazement, as the American golfer's manager, Bob Harlow, opened a suitcase stuffed with dollars – the proceeds from a series of exhibition matches – to pay a hotel bill. 'He was the fellow who made me think,' said Cotton. 'I was impressed by his way of life and I wanted to be like him.'

What Cotton had going for him was that as a former London public schoolboy he was well versed in the eccentricities of the middle class. Professional golfers, until that time, had belonged to the working class but Cotton raised the social standing of the game by ultimately becoming so famous that he was

invited to top the bill at certain theatres with a performance of trick shots.

Much is made nowadays of the top golfers' requests for appearance money – for the right to be paid a fair price for being a star attraction. Whichever side one takes, or whatever a miner deep in a pit might think of a golfer playing 72 holes with a possible reward of a million pounds-plus at the end of the rainbow – for that is what the Open can now be worth to a British winner because of extra endorsements – it is a fact that Cotton set the standards. He decided that the time had come for hard words much earlier than when he told the French, whose Open he had just won, that: 'The only way to get the best golfers is to pay for them.'

Cotton demanded, and in many cases obtained, increased prize funds but, more than anything, he

Left Henry Cotton, three times Open Champion, returns to reminisce at Royal Troon in 1982.

TONY JACKLIN

The inspiration that Jacklin found to capture the British and US Opens in the space of 11 months returned in 1985 as he cajoled his European team to their magnificent victory in the Bell's Scotch Ryder Cup at The Belfry. Jacklin's premature demise as a player was forgotten as he took the captain's role and instilled the confidence in his team members to beat the Americans for the first time since 1957. In fact Jacklin elected to back away from the fairways himself, so bringing to a rather abrupt end one of the most distinguished careers enjoyed by any British player in the game. He was actually still playing well enough to beat Bernhard Langer in a play-off for the PGA Championship at

Hillside in 1982. Thereafter, however, he looked for new challenges. Off the course he moved home to southern Spain, for business purposes, although he regularly commutes to Britain in order to commentate for the BBC.

The Jacklin story began in Scunthorpe, where he was born the son of an engine driver and learned the game that would eventually make him a national hero. His first big victories, in the Pringle Tournament and the Dunlop Masters in 1967, coincided with his arrival as a Ryder Cup player. He competed in seven successive matches as a player before becoming the captain in 1983, 1985 and then again in 1987. But there can be no doubt that the highlight of Jacklin's career came in the summer of 1969

at Royal Lytham and St Annes where he walked up the 18th fairway acknowledging the cheers of the crowd. He had become the first British winner of the Open Championship since Max Faulkner in 1953. Eleven months later he was US Open champion following a stunning win at Hazeltine. Those victories launched the golf boom in Europe, though Jacklin might have won other Open Championships if fortune had been on his side. Even so, he enjoyed a marvellous career, with 25 titles won at home and abroad in the space of 17 years, and the only thing that he lacked as a player was longevity.

Below Tony Jacklin, Britain's hero of the 1969 Open, back on top again after skippering Europe to victory in the 1985 Ryder Cup.

had the talent to support his comments. His style had its critics, for he believed that strong hands, above all, were responsible for a handsome golf shot, but he still won three Open Championships – in 1934, 1937 and 1948 – and his reputation, like that of all the truly great golfers, has endured the sands of time.

There were many who challenged Cotton during the 14 years that elapsed between his first and last Open Championship victories. But nobody over-shadowed him, so that as far as the Open was concerned it was not until Arthur D'Arcy Locke, or Bobby Locke as he was better known, of South Africa relieved Cotton of the title at Sandwich in 1949 that another era was born. And, with the decline of Cotton, so the British stranglehold on the Open was again broken. Max

Faulkner won in 1951 but it was not until Tony Jacklin triumphed in 1969 that Britain hailed another home-grown hero.

Let us, however, return to Locke. He put South Africa on the golfing map, there is no question of that, because by winning the Open in 1949, 1950, 1952 and 1957 he blazed the trail for others, notably Gary Player, from that country. As he grew older he became instantly recognizable not only because of his achievements but also because of his pot belly, which swelled out from above the plus fours which he regularly wore. He also began to hook the ball, with increasing viciousness, so that towards the end of his career he was compelled to start it out so far to the right that the ball could hurtle in the direction of unsuspecting players on an adjacent fairway before turning left towards the intended

Above Bobby Locke on the fairway during the Spalding Golf Tournament at Worthing in 1957.

Right (main picture) Bobby Locke of South Africa was the man who in 1949 took over the Open Championship title from Henry Cotton after Cotton's third and final victory the previous year. Locke is pictured competing in the Open at Royal Lytham and St Annes in 1974. (Inset) Bobby Locke wins the Open Championship for the fourth time at St Andrews in 1957.

Above Gary Player, golf's 'man in black', delivers another swinging blow.

target. But, as far as his contemporaries are concerned, there was no finer putter in the game and, for that matter, he was considered to be a master exponent of hitting the ball close from a range of within 100 yards.

Even so, Locke was a trifle fortunate to win his first Open in 1949 and more than a little lucky to

LEE TREVINO

'I didn't know my body was still capable of such things,' said the evergreen 'Merry Mex' after finishing runner-up in the 1984 Tournament Players Championship. Five months later he won the US PGA Championship! As Trevino recalled: 'I slipped from second in the money list in 1980 to 113th in 1982 because I wasn't physically capable of playing.' The reason? He had been struck by lightning in the 1975 Western Open and that led to back problems and surgery. He suffered enormous pain but never publicly complained. He simply went about his business, as well as he could, winning a tournament here and there when the pain momentarily subsided. But he went for three years from 1981 to 1984 before breaking through again, at Shoal Creek. Then at Cherry Hills twelve months later he came within a whisker of retaining the title – the last man to defend successfully was Denny Shute in 1936 and 1937 – as he finished second, only two strokes behind Hubert Green.

Trevino had by then launched another career as a television commentator, but at the 1986 US Open he finished joint fourth to emphasize that he is still very much a contender for the major championships. Born 1 December 1939, he launched his career with a victory in the 1968 US Open – he took that title again in 1971 – and he became a darling of the fairways in Britain with his buccaneer approach as he won the British Open in 1971 and 1972. In fact, he has been a frequent visitor to these shores winning, among other titles, the Benson and Hedges International and in 1985 the Dunhill British Masters. The US Masters, however, has eluded his grasp though he did win his first US PGA Championship in 1974. The captain of America's Ryder Cup team in 1985, he is regarded as one of the greatest characters in the game. As he challenged for the US Open, he said on the eve of the final round: 'My wife says she will give me a son if I win. I want that very much. I've told her that if it happens then we'll go straight home and stay in bed until Friday!'

Right Lee Trevino, winner of the Open in 1971 and 1972.

SAM TORRANCE

Years of practising on the windswept Ayrshire coast, watched by his professional father Bob, has given Sam one of the best swings in the business. The best is yet to come but Sam, since he was 'rookie of the year' on the European tour in 1972, has been a formidable golfer. There can be no doubt that his most emotional moment came when he pushed his hands high, pointing to the sky, after sinking the putt on the final green at The Belfry in 1985 which confirmed that Europe had beaten America in the Ryder Cup. Torrance is a fine team man. He has played in three Ryder Cups, five World Cups and appeared in the Hennessy Cognac, Dunhill and Nissan Cup games.

Sam was born on 24 August 1953, and his individual career took off in 1976 when he won twice in the space of six weeks, though he was compelled to wait patiently until 1979 before he scored again in the Colombian Open. That victory revived Torrance's confidence as a winner and he followed up with a fine success in the 1980 Australian PGA Championship. So, when he returned to victory in Europe capturing the Carrolls Irish Open title in 1981, there was no stopping him. Sam had a succession of triumphs, highlighted by three wins in 1984, and the key was undoubtedly his father. 'Dad knows my game inside out,' explains Sam. 'He taught me everything I know about golf and when I need to iron out a kink in my swing then a session with Dad always does the trick.' Sam relaxes by playing snooker, though when it came to celebrating the Ryder Cup win, like his team colleagues he preferred the pool – the one filled with water! There are few more emotional golfers than Sam, who proudly wears the kilt on formal occasions. And he admits: 'Winning at The Belfry was a dream come true – I was crying like a baby. It was a magical moment that I will never forget as long as I live.'

Left Sam Torrance acknowledges the cheers after securing the winning point for Europe in the 1985 Ryder Cup. 'There were tears in my eyes,' he said.

keep his fourth in 1957. He tied in 1949 with Harry Bradshaw, winning the play-off, but his Irish opponent was forever to rue an incident at the fifth hole in the second round. Bradshaw found his ball resting in a broken beer bottle and, unaware that he could have taken a free drop under the rules, he risked the splintering glass damaging his eyesight by playing the ball from where it lay. The six which he eventually marked on his card proved costly. When the play-off came, Locke, a distinguished but outspoken champion, declared that he would not compete unless new holes were cut in the greens. It was the practice in those days to keep the flags in the same position for all four rounds, but Locke's comments led to the current trend of a new hole being cut for each round.

What happened in 1957, however, could have led to an almighty inquest today, with television cameras now capturing every movement of a prospective champion, because Locke is regarded to have putted out from the wrong spot on the 18th green at St Andrews. He had been requested by Bruce Crampton, an Australian golfer, to mark his ball one clubhead's length away from where it was so that Crampton could himself putt out. Yet there are stills from a news film which indicate that when it was Locke's turn to putt he replaced the ball exactly where he had put his marker, rather than one clubhead's length back to where it had originally laid. It was, of course, an error of complete innocence and, as

it happened, Locke had only to two-putt from five feet to win. But there had been an infringement of the rules.

That victory by Locke had ended three successive wins by the Australian Peter Thomson. But Thomson returned to win in 1958, and again in 1965, although that elusive sixth victory, which would have equalled Vardon's record, remained tantalizingly out of reach.

In the 1950s the American entry was very poor. Ben Hogan, a tenacious golfer who was widely recognized as the greatest golfer of

his time, came over only once in 1953. His victory at Carnoustie was a victory of discipline and determination. Hogan, however, did not defend the championship in 1954, when Thomson won for the first time, so that by his own absence he ended the prospect of a Hogan era in the Open Championship.

Thomson, however, most certainly dominated. The paradox is that while the Americans were staying away from the Open Championship, Thomson – who had no liking for the raucous

Right Peter Thomson teeing off at the 18th hole at St Andrews during the 1984 Open.

American lifestyle – cleaned up. Thomson, a conservative dresser whose only concession to colour was to wear white shoes, felt that the American brand of golf, with well-watered greens and fairways, was too artificial. So he was more at home on the links of Britain. He favoured, too, the smaller ball, of 1.62 inches diameter, rather than the American version – 1.68 inches – which, later, would be accepted by the Royal and Ancient.

Even so, and in spite of his win in 1965, when there was a strong American representation, Thomson – perhaps because of his textbook style – could not detonate a golfing explosion. So although he won five times and Arnold Palmer scored only twice it was Palmer who revolutionized the Open at that time. For Palmer possessed the cavalier spirit to capitalize on a public in search of a golfing hero. He related to them because on the face of it his style was like their own: he stood on the first tee and hit the ball as hard as he could. In the hands of an amateur the driver might not be the safest club but it can certainly bring the most enjoyment. For everybody likes nothing more than to outdrive his opponent.

Palmer had won the US Masters and the US Open in 1960 so that summer he headed for the British Open at St Andrews. His fairways credentials matched his off-the-course reputation; he could produce winning golf while at the same time becoming the game's most popular figure. The dove-tailing of those two qualities guaranteed financial wealth for Palmer, following his link with the clever American lawyer, Mark McCormack, who realized that

Above left Past Open Champions at St Andrews in 1984. Left to right, Kel Nagle, Peter Thomson, Tony Jacklin, Gary Player, Henry Cotton, John Salvesen of the Royal and Ancient, Tom Watson (reigning champion, holding trophy), Bill Rogers, Johnny Miller, Bob Charles, Fred Daly, Lee Trevino, Arnold Palmer and Max Faulkner.

Left Royal Birkdale, scene of such a masterly stroke by Palmer in 1961 that a plaque now records his achievement there.

Left Arnold Palmer's fearless style has won him great and lasting public respect.

Below Arnold, with his wife Winnie, on winning the 1961 Open at Royal Birkdale.

since President Eisenhower had publicly demonstrated his love for golf so the sport would take off in their leisure-conscious country.

And, with Palmer's arrival at St Andrews, it also took off in Britain. He did not win in 1960, being compelled to accept second place to the American Kel Nagle, but he did in 1961 and 1962. His first triumph, at Royal Birkdale, earned him a plaque, similar to that which recorded Jones's achievement in 1926. It resulted from a shot of extraordinary strength that typified Palmer's aggressive approach. His

hallmark was surviving a crisis and, after driving into thick, heavy scrub, the only option open to him appeared to be to stab the ball back to the fairway. The thought never crossed Palmer's mind. He pulled a 6-iron from his bag and looked ahead to the green, some 140 yards away, and to the bunkers which protected it. Then he unleashed a shot of such power that the ball exploded into the air, followed by a shower of scrub, and flew to the green where it came to rest 15 feet from the hole. The risk was enormous, because the club could

have been strangled by the rough so that a smothered shot might have left the ball further embedded in the scrub. But the reward was a one-stroke win over Dai Rees, a Welshman who on three occasions was forced to settle for second place in the Open.

So Palmer became a hero, successfully defending the title twelve months later, and the Open – and the game of golf – profited. Palmer, the golfaholic, and McCormack, the workaholic, maximized the potential of the game and the Open, revitalized by Palmer's presence from the Centenary Open in 1960, regained its rightful position as the number one championship in the world.

It was extraordinary, though, that Palmer won only those two Opens. He was, of course, winning other championships in America, including four US Masters and one US Open, but on account of his talent, and his disregard of caution, he deserved more.

The problem for Palmer was the arrival of Nicklaus. Here, following

59

ROYAL ST GEORGE'S

A wild and remote links course where undulating fairways, yawning bunkers and mountainous dunes are best countered by long, straight driving.

CARD OF THE COURSE					
OUT			**IN**		
HOLE	YARDS	PAR	HOLE	YARDS	PAR
1	445	4	10	399	4
2	376	4	11	216	3
3	214	3	12	362	4
4	470	4	13	443	4
5	422	4	14	508	5
6	156	3	15	467	4
7	529	5	16	165	3
8	415	4	17	425	4
9	387	4	18	458	4
	3414	35		3443	35
			TOTAL	6857	70

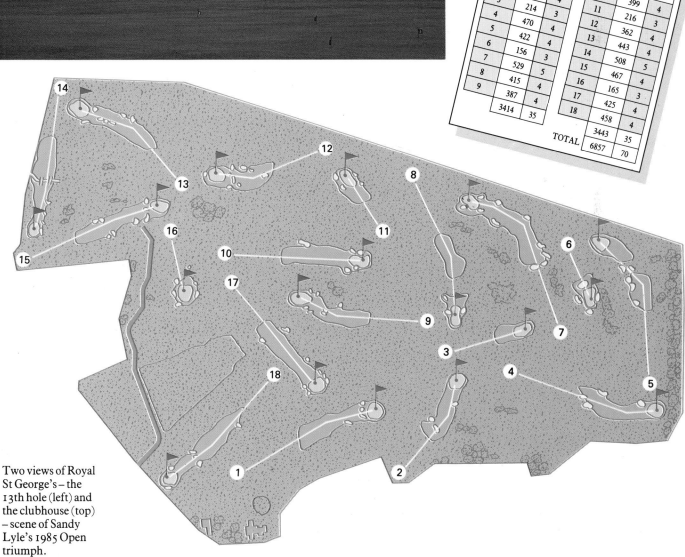

Two views of Royal St George's – the 13th hole (left) and the clubhouse (top) – scene of Sandy Lyle's 1985 Open triumph.

61

in the footsteps of Vardon, Jones and Hogan, was a master craftsman. From the age of ten Nicklaus had sought perfection, often blistering his hands as a teenager by hitting up to 500 practice shots a day, and although he lacked the charisma of Palmer he had, without any shadow of a doubt, the skill to turn the record books inside out.

That, he most certainly did. And yet the Open Championship remained, to some extent, elusive. The line between success and failure in golf is often as thin as the cover of a golf ball and, given the

Below (main picture) Muirfield was the scene of Nicklaus's Open victory in 1966. (Inset) After winning the Open Championship at St Andrews in 1970, Jack Nicklaus makes his speech.

Right Jack Nicklaus, who ruled the game for more than twenty years.

KEN BROWN

If prizes were handed out for sheer determination, then this tall, lean golfer from Harpenden, Hertfordshire, would receive his fair share. Brown's quest to become a better golfer has taken him to the US PGA Tour where he has learned to live week after week on the same fairways as the likes of Jack Nicklaus and Tom Watson. It should be said that it is love for the game that triggered his desire to seek success on the most demanding tour in the world. He could have settled for an easier, and immediately more profitable, existence in Europe. Brown won the Carris Trophy as an amateur, but little else, although he soon made his mark as a professional by earning a place in the Ryder Cup in 1977. In fact, he has not missed a Ryder Cup match since then. Brown gained his first success in the Carrolls Irish Open at Portmarnock. It provided the evidence to suggest that, as he had won on a links course, then he could be a contender for the Open Championship. In fact he made a valiant challenge at Muirfield in 1980, though the pressure of the presence of Tom Watson, the eventual winner, and Lee Trevino proved overwhelming. Brown waited until 1983 to win again, lifting the KLM Dutch Open title in Europe after winning the Benson and Hedges Kenya Open on the Safari tour. He scored again in the Glasgow Open (1984) and the Four Stars Pro-Celebrity (1985). In Europe, however, he fell from being seventh in the Order of Merit in 1983 to 29th in 1985. The reason, quite simply, was the importance he attached to competing in the United States. He struggled through 1984 and 1985, but there were signs of improvement in 1986.

Right One of Britain's most determined golfers, Ken Brown has chosen to sharpen his game on the US tour, though he is a regular contender for his country in the Ryder Cup.

odd shot here and there, Nicklaus might have won a dozen Opens. He was second no less than seven times; third on three occasions. His victories, at Muirfield in 1966, and at St Andrews in 1970 and again in 1978, were nothing less than he deserved. But still, unlike Watson, he failed to inch towards Vardon's record tally of six.

He remained, of course, the man to be beaten. And although players like Bob Charles, the left-handed New Zealander, Roberto de Vicenzo, the amiable Argentinian, Gary Player, the resilient South African, and compatriots such as Lee Trevino and Johnny Miller on occasions climbed that particular Everest in Open Championships, none emerged with the impact of Watson.

There is a lot to be said for the theory that some, like Miller and Jacklin, were simply diverted from the glory by the substantial rewards now readily available from endorsements and the like. And it would be true to say that Tom Weiskopf, who won in 1973 at Royal Troon, found the pressure of living in the Nicklaus shadow too overpowering since he was from the same town of Columbus, Ohio. Few, moreover, showed the tolerance of Player who became

Above The Argentinian player Roberto de Vicenzo became the oldest player of modern times to win the Open when, at the age of 44 years and 93 days, he succeeded at Hoylake in 1967. His score was 278.

part of the 'Big Three' with Palmer and Nicklaus, in spite of having problems commuting from his Johannesburg home in South Africa. Thus Player's achievement in winning the Open three times – in 1959, 1968 and 1974 – is all the more commendable.

The criterion of greatness, as far as the Open Championship is concerned, is the winning of it. Even those steeped in the history of the sport would struggle to recall

that J. Bulla, R. W. Horne, A. Cerda and F. Bullock are among the runners-up, since the Second World War, in the great Championship. And as Watson followed his successes in 1975 and 1977 with further victories in 1980, 1982 and 1983 it became apparent that not even Nicklaus, perhaps the greatest golfer who ever lived by virtue of his record, could keep pace with the freckle-faced Kansas City resident whom they nicknamed the 'Huckleberry Finn' of the game.

When the 1980s dawned, however, Watson was compelled to accept that across the Atlantic there was a new breed ready to fight him tooth and nail. There was Severiano Ballesteros, of Spain, the winner in 1979 and destined to be labelled the finest golfer in the world of his time. There was Bernhard Langer, of West Germany, a gutsy battler who was runner-up to Bill Rogers in the 1981 Open, and runner-up again to Ballesteros in 1984. And there was Sandy Lyle, the modest, Shropshire-based Scot who destroyed the theory that he was too nice to become an Open champion by gloriously winning the title at Royal St George's in the summer of 1985.

Ballesteros had struck his first shots, at the age of seven, with a club fashioned from a rusting 3-iron hand-fitted into a stick acting as a shaft. Langer, like Ballesteros, had been a caddie but from the moment he first saw a golf course there was to be no other occupation for him than that of professional golfer.

Lyle had hit his first shot, aged three, with a long-shafted wood. The ball travelled 80 yards – and Lyle was wearing Wellington boots at the time because he had been

Left One of the best putters of all time, the left-handed New Zealander Bob Charles won the Open in 1963 at Royal Lytham and St Annes. In the 36-hole play-off against Phil Rodgers he won by eight strokes.

SEVERIANO BALLESTEROS

Golf's most exciting gladiator and the man most likely to catch Jack Nicklaus's record of 17 major championships. Two British Opens (in 1979 at Royal Lytham and 1984 at St Andrews) and two US Masters (in 1980 and 1983) before his 28th birthday – he was born on 9 April 1957 – put him on the road. Not bad for a kid who struck his first shots at the age of seven with a club fashioned from a rusting 3-iron head hand-fitted into a stick acting as a shaft. And, as balls were too expensive, he used stones as ammunition. At age 10 he shot 51 for nine holes, and two years later he won the caddie championship at Pedrena, in northern Spain, with a spectacular 79. Since then he has won in America, Britain, Holland, France, Switzerland, Germany, Scandinavia, Ireland, Japan, New Zealand, Kenya, Australia, South Africa and, of course, his native Spain.

His prolific winning spell began at the age of 19 only two weeks after he had displayed his rich potential by leading the British Open at Royal Birkdale in 1976, where only Johnny Miller eventually finished ahead of him. It was a

disappointing finish for the young Spaniard, who was convinced even at that age that he was capable of winning major championships, but he soon blossomed as he took the Dutch Open title. In fact, he rocketed to the top of the Order of Merit in 1976 and he held that position with three European titles in 1977 and then again with four in 1978. He is of golfing stock as his uncle is Ramón Sota, the veteran World Cup golfer who once finished sixth in the US Masters. Like his three brothers – Baldomero, Vicente and Manuel – he made golf his life . . . all four learning the game on the

Real Club of Pedrena on Spain's rugged northern coast, close to the port of Santander. Seve, however, progressed to being the finest player in the world. He followed a tremendous season in 1985 – winning five times in Europe – with another great year in 1986. He quickly captured titles like the Dunhill British Masters and the Carrolls Irish Open (for a third time in four years) as he concentrated on challenging for the number one spot in Europe again after being banned from the US PGA Tour for not competing in the mandatory 15 events in 1985.

Right It's there! Seve sinks the winning putt in the 1984 Open at St Andrews, his second Open victory. He scored 276, beating Watson and Langer by two strokes.

Left Sandy Lyle takes a one-stroke lead in the 1985 British Open and acknowledges the crowd's delight. That one stroke was sufficient for Lyle to become the new champion taking the title from Seve Ballesteros.

realized that golf was his natural talent; Ballesteros, by the very nature of his upbringing, made that decision much earlier.

And Lyle? He was of golfing stock. His grandfather, a farmer, left his land, some seven miles north-west of Glasgow, to his nine children. There, three of the brothers – Alex, Sandy's father, Walter and George – carved out the Clober course where George remained the professional.

Alex Lyle moved south to take up a professional-cum-greenkeeping job at Hawkstone

helping his father, Alex, the professional at the Hawkstone Park Country Club in Shropshire, to siphon water off the greens.

Initially Ballesteros dominated. He became the new favourite, ousting Watson as the American struggled with his game, and, more importantly, outgunning him in an exhilarating contest at St Andrews in 1984. In a sense Watson and Ballesteros had formed their own era. Now, for a while, it was 'Goliath' against 'Goliath'. They might have come from vastly different backgrounds but for them the ambition was the same – to seek universal acclaim and immortalization. To be compared with the greats of the modern era, with the likes of Nicklaus and Palmer, meant a lot; but to be linked with the likes of Braid,

Taylor and Vardon was to be part of the game's history.

In Ballesteros there is much to be compared with Vardon. For Vardon played his first shots with a club which consisted of a blackthorn branch as a shaft, an oak branch as a head and a strip of tin as a face. He used a white marble as a ball.

Watson, at the age of six, struck his first shots in considerably more affluent surroundings. He caddied for his father at the private club near their home while Ballesteros forged his links with the game working for 25 pence a round as a caddie. Watson went on to study at Stanford University, where he graduated in psychology, on the way, or so it seemed, to a career in insurance. It was four years later, when in his twenties, that he

Park, near Shrewsbury. There, in 1958, Sandy was born. In his first official medal card, at the age of nine, he scored 124. He broke 80 at the age of 10. He was a Boy international at the age of 14. And he won several prestigious amateur titles and became a Walker Cup player, representing Great Britain and Ireland against the United States, before turning professional.

Yet, despite becoming the leader of the European Order of Merit in 1979 and 1980, he somehow lived in the shadow of Nick Faldo. It did not help Lyle that in 1983 he lost

an 11-shot lead with 22 holes to play against Faldo in the European Masters.

Then, at Royal St George's, Lyle became Britain's first Open champion since Tony Jacklin. The first three rounds had unfolded to leave Australia's David Graham and the West German Langer sharing the lead three strokes ahead of their nearest rivals, who included Lyle.

The swing which brought Lyle home as champion came at the 14th, where he holed a monster putt for a birdie four, and at the

15th where he successfully made a 14-foot putt for a rare birdie at that hole. Lyle, inevitably, provided the spectators around the 18th green, and millions watching on television, with cause to hold their breath in disbelief. His second shot had run away to the left into 'Duncan's Hollow' where in 1922 George Duncan had failed to get up and down in two to force a play-off with Walter Hagen. Lyle's chip refused to climb over the shelf halfway up the green and the ball trickled back. He two-putted from there but he now faced an anxious 30 minutes, along with the patriotic crowd, to see if either Graham or Langer could catch him. They did not.

So Lyle was crowned champion. He had scored a last round of 70 for a two over par winning aggregate of 282 – one shot ahead of the American Payne Stewart.

Ballesteros and Watson were back in the pack, and a further Open victory was to elude them yet again in 1986 when, of course, Lyle lost his title to Greg Norman. In 1987 the Americans will be keener than ever, although Ballesteros, Lyle and Norman will be just as eager to repel their invasion once more.

Left Tom Watson meets his Waterloo at the infamous 17th 'Road' hole at St Andrews in 1984. Ballesteros won his second Open that year, and Watson and Langer were joint runners-up. Victory for Watson would have given him a hat-trick of British Open wins which was last achieved by the Australian Peter Thomson (1954-6).

FALDO ON FAIRWAY WOODS

If you have accepted my recommendation that an amateur should disregard the driver then it follows that there is more room in the bag for other clubs. I suggest that the space is filled with another wood and, indeed, that the 3-iron is cast aside in favour of yet another wood, for there is little doubt that the 6- and 7-woods, which are becoming increasingly popular, are a major asset to the average amateur. If you are a real beginner then I would put 3-, 5-, 6- and 7-woods in your bag and, if you wish to lighten the load, leave out both the 3- and 4-irons.

Of course, as with anything in golf, it is a matter of personal preference but I have no hesitation in stressing that everybody should move towards having 6- and 7-woods in their bag. Even so, there is still a need to be somewhat cautious. There is no question that the 6- and 7-woods, with their extreme lofts, can be employed to fire a ball out of the rough. They sweep through the grass more easily than an iron, and by increasing the likelihood of a pure contact they make it more probable that the ball will reach the green. The trouble stems from a player discovering he can achieve such a result and then believing that he can repeat this success time and time

again. It does not work out that way.

You cannot always go wading into shin-high rough, armed with your 7-wood, and expect to succeed with your shot because if there is tangled grass all the way behind the ball they you will simply not obtain that pure contact. You would not obtain it with a 3-iron, probably not with a 6-iron and maybe not even with an 8-iron. For there are moments in this game when you must accept that you have to pay the penalty for a wayward shot and that penalty is to play safe.

I have seen quite a few amateurs take out the wood and top the ball, take out the wood again and scuttle the ball along the ground again, then, in frustration, swing with all their might and send the ball crashing into the trees. A medal card, one in which every score counts, has then been ruined or the prospect of a point being salvaged on

a stableford card has been lost or, in match play, an opponent has been handed a hole without needing to fight for it.

So do not become too ambitious with the fairway woods. Use them wherever possible, because they will be an asset to your game, but remember at all times the art of course management which, if learnt correctly, will enable you to save up to six shots each round.

Meanwhile, persevere with obtaining a smooth swing because there is nothing quite like hitting a 3-wood off a fairway and watching the ball sail through the air and on to the green more than 200 yards away from you. The fairway woods have broad soles and these encourage the club to slide across the playing surface so that you can think in terms of sweeping the ball on its way and allowing the extreme loft to get the ball airborne rather than trying to achieve this with a scooping action.

Left A smooth swing ensures a satisfactory shot.

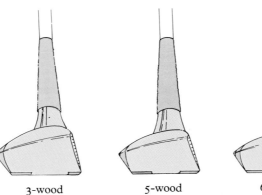

3-wood   5-wood

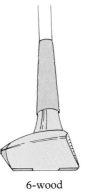

6-wood

7-wood

CHAPTER TWO
A NATIONAL INSTITUTION

CHAPTER TWO

A NATIONAL INSTITUTION –

the US Masters Tournament

There are moments in sport which, unquestionably, leave the spectator as emotionally exhausted as the participant. In the 1986 Gold Cup the sight of indomitable jockey Jonjo O'Neill galvanizing that game mare Dawn Run to a glorious last gasp success left not a dry eye in the Cheltenham house. Dawn Run, however, was the favourite. One month later, at Augusta, as revered a place to the golfing fraternity as Cheltenham is to steeplechasing enthusiasts, Jack Nicklaus started as an outsider, remained that way for 63 holes of the US Masters, then rolled back the years to gain a memorable triumph. If there is a purist of the game around who did not shed a tear or two as Nicklaus's victory was confirmed, then I have yet to find him.

Consider the facts before examining the performance which enabled Nicklaus to return to Augusta in 1987 seeking his seventh US Masters title. He arrived at the Augusta National Golf Club on Monday, April 7, 1986, as the winner of the princely sum of $4,404 so far that season. He was 160th in the US PGA Tour official money list, with the dubious record of having completed only three of the seven events in which he had competed.

Previous spread Bernhard Langer at the 1985 US Masters, only seconds away from victory.

Right 'We could take it in a little at the shoulders, sir,' Langer seems to be saying as Jack Nicklaus dons the green jacket.

What is more, Nicklaus had not won a major championship since 1980. In six years he had won only two tour events. His contemporaries, including those players who had dared to challenge him over the last two decades, were now pointing an accusing finger at Nicklaus. They claimed that he, or his hands at least, had gone soft through lack of practice and that he spent more time holding a telephone, co-ordinating the affairs of his far-flung business empire, than gripping a club. The time had arrived, they felt, not so much to bury him but at least to praise him for all his achievements, since he could evidently never recapture the glories of the good old days.

Anyway, at 46 years of age a man cannot possibly win a major championship. Or can he? Hadn't

Julius Boros, an American of Hungarian extraction, rolled back the years in 1968 by winning the US PGA Championship at the age of 48? He claimed, as he prepared for the final round, that he had no chance of winning.

Nicklaus, however, did not feel altogether uncomfortable about his position as he left the practice putting green, surrounded by his supporters, and zig-zagged his way through the crowd to the first tee. He had spoken by telephone to Steve, one of his three sons, the evening before and they agreed that a final round of 65 might do the trick. As he stood there, with his eldest son Jack Jnr by his side as his caddie, not even Nicklaus could have imagined the fairytale that would unfold that afternoon.

Greg Norman, the luckless

Above In the centre background, Seve Ballesteros (black trousers) and Jack Nicklaus (brown trousers) leaving the 7th tee during the 1984 Masters.

Australian, would be teeing off some 30 minutes later as the leader. He had scored rounds of 70, 72 and 68 to be on 210, six under par, and he led by one stroke from defending champion Bernhard Langer, Severiano Ballesteros, South Africa's Nick Price, who had broken the course record the previous day with a 63, and the inexperienced American Donnie Hammond. Tom Kite, Tom Watson and Japan's Tommy Nakajima were one stroke further adrift; Nicklaus was one of a group of players on 214.

The bookmakers back in London were still convinced that Nicklaus

73

was a forlorn hope. They marked him up as a 28-1 outsider that Sunday morning as the money rained down on the back of Ballesteros. The bookmakers are undoubtedly more accustomed to interpreting the ability of a Dawn Run but on this occasion there seemed no reason to assume, as the golfers passed through the eighth hole, that they had not been anything but wholly justified in shortening the Spaniard's price to 7-4.

Number eight on the Augusta course measures 535 yards and as it is an uphill affair it plays every inch of that distance. It has, however, been dominated in the past. Claude Harmon, a native of Georgia, reached the green in two in 1948 and after holing his putt for an eagle three he moved on to win the tournament.

There was to be no eagle for Nicklaus. He saw to that himself by leaking his drive out to the right so that the ball finished under the towering Georgia pines. Ballesteros, however, came along a few minutes later and contrived to hole a pitch shot of fully 45 yards for an unlikely eagle three. Within seconds everybody walking the course, on and off the fairways, realized that the Spaniard was ahead as the name of Ballesteros moved to the top of the list on the giant leader-boards.

Yet it is worth returning to that eighth hole. For it was there, albeit with a par five, that Nicklaus undoubtedly sparked off what was to be one of his greatest charges. There, beneath those pines, he studied the path ahead looking for a means of escape. And it was there that Nicklaus decided to throw caution to the wind, discarding all thoughts of playing a conservative recovery. He looked up at the spectators gathered around him and, with a wink and a wry smile, pulled his three wood from the bag.

Fate was kind to Nicklaus. This was a reckless gamble, and from the look on his face he knew it, but he drew the club back smoothly and then swung himself almost off

Below Seve Ballesteros came to grief at the 15th hole on the Augusta course during the 1986 US Masters.

SAM SNEAD

Born in Hot Springs, Virginia, on 27 May 1912, he is credited with having scored 135 victories. No less than 84 – a record – of those came on the US PGA Tour, the first in the 1936 Virginia Closed event and the last in the 1965 Greensboro Open. He was British Open champion in 1946, US Masters champion in 1949, 1952 and 1954 and US PGA Champion in 1942, 1949 and 1951. But he never won the US Open, finishing runner-up on four occasions. He has had no less than 24 holes in one!

Snead, a member of the World Golf Hall of Fame, is so flexible that even at the age of 70 he displayed his agility by kicking his foot high enough to touch the top section of a door surround. But he was not so flexible with his feelings at the 1969 Ryder Cup. There Jack Nicklaus conceded a putt of three feet to Tony Jacklin on the last green so that the match was halved . . . and so that Jacklin did not face the terrifying experience of facing one putt to decide the issue. It was a most charitable gesture on Nicklaus's part but Snead was annoyed that it had been made.

Sam Snead devised his unique putting style as a means of overcoming the 'yips' – an inability to sink short putts. He originally putted between his legs, croquet style. When this was banned, however, he modified his stance to that shown here, in which his feet are together and the ball is ahead of his right toe.

Right Sam Snead putting on the style.

Right The smile on Jack Nicklaus's face grows broader after yet another birdie putt *en route* to his 1986 US Masters victory.

Suddenly, Nicklaus was like a little kid let loose on his own in the sweet shop. He ran back to the fairway, joyously exchanging words with his son, and could not stop himself chattering about his miracle shot with playing partner Sandy Lyle.

From that moment on there was to be no stopping the 'Golden Bear'. If we take Nicklaus and Ballesteros through the eighth, then we have the American six shots behind the Spaniard with ten holes to play. The next couple of hours have been well documented. Nicklaus went on to birdie the ninth and he packed five birdies and one eagle into an inward half of 30. He had completed the 65 that he had predicted would be enough, but now he was compelled to wait back in the clubhouse with his nine-under-par aggregate of 279 on the board.

Nicklaus was aware that Ballesteros had gathered another eagle at the long 13th. Yet he still believed that the Spaniard might slip on a banana skin or two over the closing stretch. So it proved. Ballesteros struck an uncharacteristic four-iron approach towards a watery grave at the long 15th, where he marked a six on his card, and then three-putted the 17th to lose all chance of winning the title for a third time.

Nicklaus could still be beaten. First Kite, then Norman, who had pulled his way back into contention with four successive birdies from the 14th, had putts of 15 feet to take Nicklaus into a play-off. Both missed – and Nicklaus, who had hugged his son Jack as they left the 18th green, now turned to his wife, Barbara, with tears in his eyes.

He had won the US Masters for the sixth time in his career, firmly distancing himself from the four

his feet. Nicklaus, almost disbelieving, closed his eyes – listening intently for the faintest click that would tell him the ball had been deflected back into

trouble – and as the seconds past without a sound, he knew that the ball had somehow threaded its way through the branches to the sanctuary of the fairway.

wins of Arnold Palmer, the three wins of Jimmy Demaret, Gary Player and Sam Snead, and the double wins of Ballesteros, Ben Hogan, Byron Nelson, Horton Smith and Tom Watson. The roll-call of winners is a veritable *Who's Who* of golf, for Billy Casper, Ben Crenshaw, Raymond Floyd, Gene Sarazen and Fuzzy Zoeller are five other winners fortunate enough to have earned the famous 'Green Jacket' which is traditionally awarded to the champion.

One year and five days prior to Nicklaus's victory, what odds would a bookmaker have been prepared to offer that in 1986 a West German, who confessed that barely more than 13 years earlier he knew nothing about Nicklaus, would be the defeated champion helping his successor into the green jacket? For in 1985, against all the odds, Bernhard Langer had won

the 49th US Masters. He won it in style with four birdies in the last seven holes. With that marvellous flourish he transformed this particular production into

compelling viewing as the American Curtis Strange, four ahead with nine holes to play, lost his way over the closing stretch.

Ecstasy for Langer, however, meant agony for most Americans. The Masters is a part of their sporting heritage and for the fourth time in eight years it had been removed from their grasp by an overseas player. Even so, there is every reason for thinking that Robert Tyre Jones Jr, who created the US Masters, would have welcomed Langer's triumph. Jones won 13 major championships in all, including achieving the Grand Slam in 1930 which in those days comprised the Open and Amateur Championships of Britain and America. But he was much more than simply an astonishing golfer. He was a gentleman with an affectionate nature who loved the game and his fellow competitors. Moreover he appreciated the value of inviting foreign players.

The story goes that Gary Player's father wrote to Bobby Jones in the mid-1950s eulogizing the golfing talent of his son. Mr Player stated that he could not afford to pay Gary's way from South Africa to America but that if an invitation was forthcoming then he would pass the hat among his friends. The reply from Augusta was genuine and succinct: 'Pass the hat.'

So the young Gary Player made his début in the Masters. Then in 1961, at the age of 25, he became the first foreign entry to capture the championship. Player, by now established as a world-class golfer following his victory in the Open Championship in 1959, salvaged a par four from out of a bunker at the 18th green in the last round. Moments later Arnold Palmer took six from the same bunker to lose the title by one stroke.

Above right West Germany's Bernhard Langer won his first major championship when he took the US Masters at Augusta in 1985.

Right Gary Player splashes out of a bunker during the 1985 US Masters.

Palmer's four wins, of course, were instrumental in establishing the Masters as the first-leg championship in the modern-day Grand Slam. From its inception in 1934, the Masters was played early in the year, in March, to coincide with the sportswriters from the big daily newspapers returning north following their annual pilgrimage to Florida each spring where they watched the baseball season get under way at the training camps.

In fact it was those reporters rather than Jones who christened the championship. Jones, the

'At all times I have been conscious of a beautiful golf course, one that demands the utmost in skill and intelligence. The Augusta National is one of the few courses that can give me real pleasure in playing the day after the tournament ends.'

Ben Hogan on the Augusta National Course

greatest amateur golfer in the history of the game, had retired at the age of 28, following his Grand Slam performance, to concentrate on his business interests. Golf, however, was in his blood and he had one burning desire: to build a golf course where he could play with his friends.

In Augusta, some 100 miles from his home in Atlanta, Georgia, there was a nursery known as 'Fruitlands' which was for sale at Depression prices. It had been developed in 1857 by Dr L. E. M. Berckmans, a Belgian horticulturist, and when Jones viewed the 365 acres he immediately realized that he had the perfect site. He said: 'When I walked out on the grass terrace under the big trees behind the house and looked down over the property the experience was unforgettable. It seemed that this land had been lying here for years just waiting for someone to lay a golf course upon it.'

As luck would have it, at some time beforehand Jones had played on the newly designed Cypress Point course, on California's rugged coast, which had been the work of the Scottish physician Dr Alister Mackenzie. For Mackenzie, of course, it had been like being at home, since the topography was similar to that of Scottish linksland, and at Cypress he created a masterpiece. Bobby Jones had been impressed, very impressed.

So his first thought on purchasing 'Fruitlands' was to contact Mackenzie. By now the finance was available because Clifford Roberts, a New York investment banker, had befriended Jones and he, too, wanted a place where he could play the game unhurriedly and in quiet seclusion with his friends. Roberts it was

who fashioned the Masters; but it was Mackenzie, forming a sympathetic 'marriage' with Jones, who lovingly created the course for the Augusta National Golf Club. It was to become the only permanent site for one of the world's major championships.

Jones, however, never visualized the Masters becoming *the* Masters. His desire was to have a tournament for his friends and that is how the championship came into being in 1934 as the Augusta National Invitation Tournament. One of the participants, Horton Smith, already had a number of tournament and financial successes behind him, and since Smith won that year, when Jones finished joint 13th himself, the sports-writers insisted on calling it 'the Masters'. Thus the championship outgrew its origins while still in its embryonic state.

Jones, however, witnessed the moment – or rather the shot – that

Left Arnold Palmer still going strong at the 1985 US Masters with four wins behind him.

Above 1981 at Augusta and Gene Sarazen takes a walk down memory lane.

instantly gave the Masters international prestige. The 15th hole, a long, tortuous par five, provided the scene. Craig Wood, edged out by Smith the previous year, was by now back in the cloistered clubhouse being acclaimed the second Masters champion. But at the 15th Gene Sarazen pulled a 4-wood from his bag and rifled the ball from 220 yards towards the green. It finished in the hole for that rarest golfing 'bird' of all – an albatross two. History has proclaimed Sarazen's shot as being heard around the world and others have insisted that the cheer that went up from around the green most certainly was. In fact there were only 25 people there at the time and one of them was Jones. Thus Sarazen tied and went on to beat the luckless Wood in a play-off.

Sarazen had provided the Masters with its birthright. The sportswriters flashed their messages of his astonishing shot across America and, more importantly, across the world. But it was not until 1938, when Henry Picard won, that Jones and Roberts announced that 'the public has accepted the Masters by name and the club, like the press, now adopts it.'

Roberts was also instrumental in changing the date of the Championship from March to April so that there was more chance of the thousands of towering pine trees, which line the fairways, being punctuated by a profusion of colour with the pink, red and white of the azaleas and dogwood. The course provides a kind of chess-game examination for the players because, in spite of the wide fairways, it is important to think one or two shots ahead so as to drive the ball into a place from where it is best to attack the pin. There is little rough and few bunkers. Jones was insistent that the course should not severely punish the wayward shot but should offer a reward to the player who could produce the kind of approach that would give him the opportunity of putting for a birdie on the fast, undulating greens.

Like any other great championship, however, the Masters relies on the players to provide the real drama. As in a theatre there are times when an anticipatory atmosphere hangs over the course. The crowd is spellbound, and an eerie silence seems to herald a triumph or a tragedy. Then, more often than not, a sudden explosion of excitement signals a moment of glory.

After the Second World War the dapper Jimmy Demaret and the machine-like Ben Hogan – two former caddies from Texas – and the straw-hatted Sam Snead consigned most of the other players to the roles of supporting cast. The modern age, however, began in 1958 when Palmer won the first of his four Masters. He was then 28 years old and he became the youngest champion since Byron Nelson who won at the age of 25 in 1937.

Palmer enriched the game, and especially the Masters, with his swashbuckling approach. He hitched up his trousers and attacked Augusta like no player before him had been prepared to do. Thus Arnie's 'Army' was born and his troops, hypnotized by his charisma, cried 'Charge' as Palmer won alternate Masters through to 1964. His performance of leading at the end of each day in the 1960 Masters was an example of his ability to handle the special pressures that exist when the rest of the field are snapping at your heels. Even so he was one behind Ken Venturi, with two holes to play, before he discovered the inspiration to birdie both the 17th and 18th to win by the narrowest of margins.

In 1962 there was even greater drama. Palmer had to chip in for a two at the short 16th then birdie the 17th in order to force a play-off

Above In 1962 there was a play-off between Player (above), Palmer and Finsterwald; Palmer triumphed.

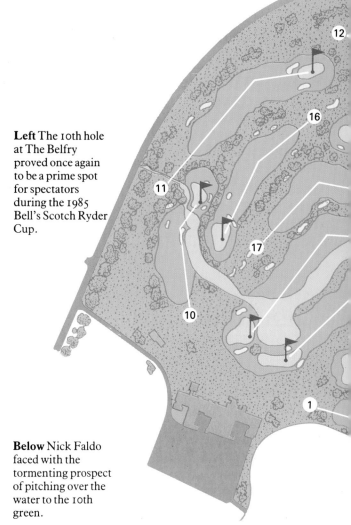

Left The 10th hole at The Belfry proved once again to be a prime spot for spectators during the 1985 Bell's Scotch Ryder Cup.

Below Nick Faldo faced with the tormenting prospect of pitching over the water to the 10th green.

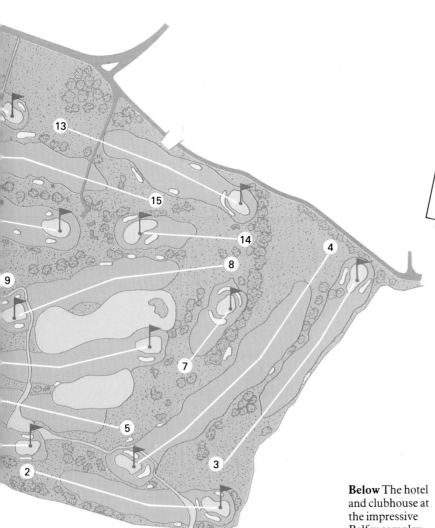

CARD OF THE COURSE						
OUT				**IN**		
HOLE	YARDS	PAR		HOLE	YARDS	PAR
1	408	4		10	301	4
2	340	4		11	365	4
3	455	4		12	225	3
4	569	5		13	364	4
5	389	4		14	184	3
6	386	4		15	540	5
7	173	3		16	400	4
8	476	5		17	555	5
9	390	4		18	455	4
	3586	37			3389	36
			TOTAL		6975	73

THE BELFRY

Set in parkland, the Brabazon course is now regarded as a premier inland course, with most of its holes being approached over streams.

Below The hotel and clubhouse at the impressive Belfry complex.

AUGUSTA

Swinging round the US Masters venue

Hole 1: *Very good, as an opener, with a bunker right side of the fairway at about 245 yards, narrowing the fairway. A good drive will leave something between a 7- and 9-iron to the green which has an undulating tier, running S-shape back right to front left. The green, of course, is well guarded by bunkers.*

Hole 2: *The ideal drive is to draw the ball down the fairway avoiding a large trap on the right at about 270 to 280 yards. The second shot is extremely difficult, off a downslope. You can go for the green or hit an iron, calculating where to land so that you have a full sand wedge into the green which slopes from back to front. The green is well guarded by bunkers.*

Hole 3: *Usually a 1-iron or 3-wood is right for position off the tee. The idea is to miss the bunker on the left, then have an 8- or 9-iron into the green. The green is L-shaped and it's best to land the ball on the left side, although it is not very deep in that area, so as to have an uphill putt for a birdie chance. But it is a hard green to keep the ball on and it is easy to go over the back.*

Hole 4: *The first par three, which is played from an elevated tee, through a big gulley with a 3- or 4-iron, to a green that is especially well guarded by a bunker front right. It is not much of a hole – but it is all carry. You can hit the green and roll back off.*

Hole 5: *The land goes uphill again here, so you need to hit a long, drawing drive. The fairway is about 60 yards wide but it is best to hug the left side because from there you*

have a better view of a slightly elevated green, with a tier running through it and a dangerous trap back left. You're going in with anything between a 2- and a 5-iron and it is very easy to leak the ball slightly right, which can leave you with a delicate pitch from the edge or a long, fast, breaking putt.

Hole 6: *Another downhill par three to a green which has a very small plateau at the back right, which is where they often put the pin. There is a massive front tier, something like the third at Wentworth, and if the ball goes anywhere near that then it will come off and roll right down to the front. The first putt is always very difficult unless you get the tee shot close.*

Hole 7: *A nice hole through the trees, and as there is a flat spot on the fairway at about 220 yards it is wise to take something like a 2-iron and aim for it, so as to leave yourself a good position. Then it's an 8-iron. It is a little dangerous to try and hit a 3-wood as you can get the ball too close to the overhanging branches. The elevated green is well guarded by bunkers with a small tier running through it from the front to the back left. The right half of the green is a good three feet lower.*

Hole 8: *You drive up the hill here, seeking to miss a big trap on the right at about 260 yards and hoping not to leak the ball out to the right into the trees. From the fairway it's another wood, although this is a blind shot so you take aim on the pine trees in the distance. The hole turns sharp left at the end and you are usually faced with a pitch shot of between 60 and 100 yards to a green which has three large humps on the left.*

Hole 9: *The hole dives downwards into a big dip then rises again to the green. You hope for a flat lie after a big drive, in order to get a good shot into the green. This is not as fierce as it was, as they have taken some of the slope out of it. In the past it was relatively common to see a ball hit the green and spin back off or even to see a putt roll straight off the green, but that did not occur so much in 1986.*

Left A panoramic shot of the clubhouse at Augusta National with spectators at the 18th (left) and 9th greens just beyond.

Right Visitors walking through a botanical garden in America? No – just spectators in the vicinity of the 6th hole at Augusta National.

Hole 10: *There is a marvellous view down the hill from the tee – but there is little time to think about that! You have to nail the drive, drawing it from right to left, so that the ball gets over a plateau and runs down the hill. If you do that, then it's a 4- or 5-iron in; if you don't, then you could be going in with a 5-wood.*

The second shot, however, is one of the most beautiful in golf, with a bunker 60 yards short of the green, making sure that you cannot leave anything to chance. The green is quite big and flat in the middle,

although it falls away at the far left side.

Hole 11: *A very generous fairway so that you can choose to draw or fade the ball. Then you hit the*

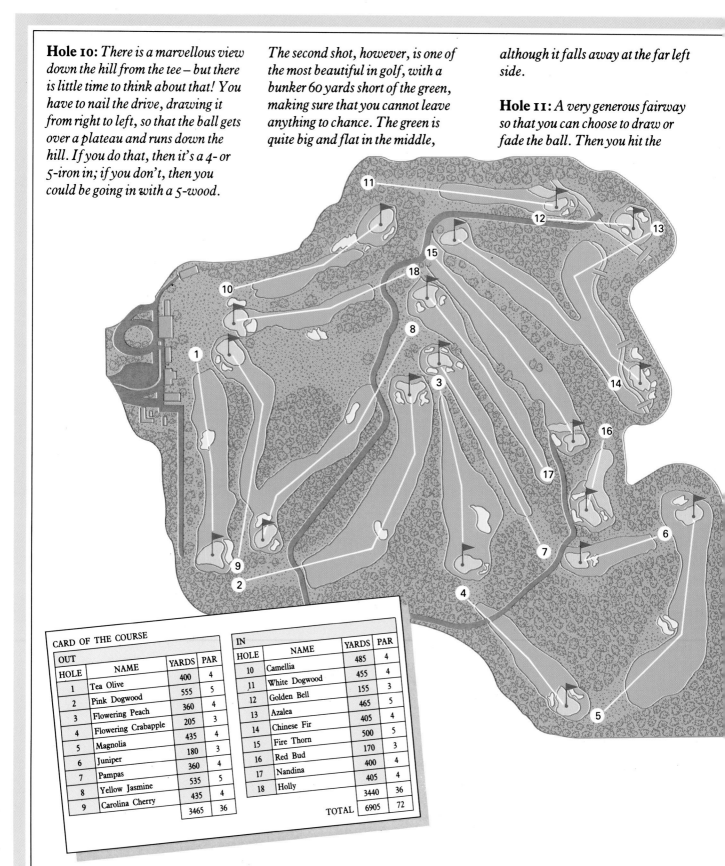

CARD OF THE COURSE			
OUT			
HOLE	NAME	YARDS	PAR
1	Tea Olive	400	4
2	Pink Dogwood	555	5
3	Flowering Peach	360	4
4	Flowering Crabapple	205	3
5	Magnolia	435	4
6	Juniper	180	3
7	Pampas	360	4
8	Yellow Jasmine	535	5
9	Carolina Cherry	435	4
		3465	36

IN			
HOLE	NAME	YARDS	PAR
10	Camellia	485	4
11	White Dogwood	455	4
12	Golden Bell	155	3
13	Azalea	465	5
14	Chinese Fir	405	4
15	Fire Thorn	500	5
16	Red Bud	170	3
17	Nandina	400	4
18	Holly	405	4
		3440	36
	TOTAL	6905	72

second along a line following the water, which runs up the left then edges in towards the green. The green is very fast, so you don't really want to miss on the right as you could chip and watch the ball run all the way through and into the water. There are a couple of bunkers at the rear of the green.

Hole 12: *The difficulty here is in selecting the right club, with the wind swirling around you. It is easier than you can imagine to dump the tee shot into the water fronting the green. Easy, too, to hit the pitch from the dropping zone into the water or the front bunker, which provides the green with further protection. This is one of the great par threes of the world and it has ruined many a player's prospects of winning the Masters.*

Hole 13: *It is important to draw the ball in order to get the distance to be able to go for the green in two. But if you pull the ball too far from right to left, then it can roll down the sloping fairway into Rae's creek. The creek goes up the left side of the green then cuts across the front so that a number of players have found a watery grave trying to reach the green with their second shot. If you do lay up then it is important to have a full second shot into the green, which has been remodelled with a swale behind it.*

Hole 14: *I think a majority of the professionals take a 3-wood here and a good one leaves a straightforward 8-iron to a green which is one of the fastest on the course, with a multitude of contours. It slopes from left to right and there are all kinds of*

humps and hollows, tiers and plateaux.

Hole 15: *You stand there and let it rip off the tee. All you've got! It's a generous fairway and the further you hit the ball, then the better the chance of getting to the green in two. I have always had a 5-wood in the bag for Augusta and it is a useful club for the second shot here. The green is the other side of a lake although TV viewers will probably not appreciate that there is water beyond the green.*

Hole 16: *Another famous TV shot across the water. The idea is to land the ball to the right side of the green but slightly left of a little ridge, so that the ball immediately breaks left and runs down to the bottom where the pin is most often put. If the green is running very fast, then the ball could run out of land and topple into a bunker or into the water. The hole really penalizes an off-target shot, whether you go right or left. Go right and you could be bunkered and*

Above The 15th green at Augusta where Sarazen scored an albatross two in 1935 and went on to win.

splashing out towards the water. Go left and you will land in the water!

Hole 17: *A reasonably straightforward hole. The tee shot, with either a 3-wood or a 1-iron, must be guided between trees leaving a short iron into a slightly raised green, which has lots of contours again and rolls off slightly to the left.*

Hole 18: *You drive uphill at this hole, back towards the clubhouse, with the generous fairway narrowed at the landing area by bunkers on the left and trees on the right. The second shot must be struck positively as it is easy to leak the ball out to the right and finish in a bunker or, if you are wide of it, from a position where it is difficult to get the ball close. It is a good finishing hole – one that puts all the pressure on making a four if victory in the US Masters is in sight.*

with Dow Finsterwald and Player. In the 18-hole play-off, the following day, Player seemed to be in command. But at the 10th the yell of 'Charge' erupted as Palmer nursed home a putt of fully 40 feet for a birdie. He responded with four more birdies during an inward 31 which gave him a score of 68 – three better than Player. Finsterwald toiled to a 77.

Palmer's dominance was eventually broken by the emergence of a tubby individual by the name of Jack Nicklaus. He won in 1963 then again in 1965 and 1966. The Palmer fans displayed their infuriation by standing in trees and bushes holding crudely written cards like 'Hit the ball here, fat boy'. Nicklaus, however, was never intimidated. In 1965 he overpowered his rivals as he won by nine shots with a record aggregate of 271 which is 17 under par. Afterwards Jones said: 'Jack Nicklaus is playing an entirely different game – a game I'm not even familiar with.'

Then as Nicklaus shed pound after pound, growing a mane of blond hair so that he became known as the 'Golden Bear', the crowds began to appreciate his remarkable skills. To use a cliché he became the master of the Masters, winning again in 1972 and 1975. Sadly, Jones did not live to see these two victories. He had been confined to a wheelchair for a great many years, because of a wasting disease, although he had visited St Andrews in 1958 to receive the Freedom of the City. He died in 1971.

Below The 16th at Augusta where Palmer chipped in for two in 1962.

JACK NICKLAUS

Recognized as the greatest golfer ever and with a record of 20 major championships – 18 professional and two amateur – to prove it, the 'Golden Bear' has won six US Masters, five US PGA Championships, four US Opens, three British Opens and two US Amateur Championships. In spite of that, it has been a common experience for him to find himself 'written-off' by the golfing media. It is questionable, however, whether anyone will be brave enough to do so again following his great comeback in 1986. Nicklaus had gone six years without winning a major championship – and two years without a victory of any description – when he defied logic by storming out of the pack in typical fashion to win the US Masters at Augusta for a record sixth time. Nicklaus, whose son Jackie, a fine golfer himself, acted as caddie, was overcome with emotion as he putted the life out of Augusta's last nine holes and out of his rivals. It was a performance which emphasized what all Americans, and all the rest of the world's golf observers, feel: there will never be another Jack William Nicklaus.

That success at Augusta took his victories on the US PGA Tour to 71

– only Sam Snead has won more. But Nicklaus, PGA Player of the Year five times and number one in the official money list on no fewer than eight occasions, has also won the Australian Open six times, though he has rarely competed in Britain outside of the Open Championship. Born in Columbus, Ohio, on 21 January 1940, he runs the huge Golden Bear Inc. company which has a gross income of 200 million dollars a year and has, during his career, won more than five million dollars in official money. He initially struggled to gain the love of the American public, as he began to put down their hero Arnold Palmer, but he finally won their hearts. And you can be sure that Augusta, in 1986, was certainly no place for weak hearts!

Right In a class of his own, Jack Nicklaus – whose nickname is the 'Golden Bear'. His use of the interlocking grip is well illustrated here. The forefinger of the left hand is linked with the little finger of the right so that the hands are firmly united.

Even Nicklaus, however, was compelled to make way for another era – that of Tom Watson and Seve Ballesteros – before he returned to remind them of his extraordinary talents with a record sixth win in 1986. Nicklaus had launched another tremendous challenge in 1977 by gathering seven birdies in the last round but when Watson holed from 20 feet at the 17th for a birdie it provided too much of a hurdle for even Nicklaus to overcome. Thus Watson won for the first time and he was to take the title again in 1981. Fuzzy Zoeller broke an Augusta hoodoo by winning at his first attempt in 1979, scoring a birdie at the second extra hole in the first sudden-death play-off to beat Watson and Ed Sneed, and Craig Stadler was another 'extra time' winner against Dan Pohl in 1982.

The Americans' exclusive hold on the title, however – previously broken only by Player – was now being challenged. It was Player, again, who had won in 1978 when he produced an amazing last round of 64 which at that time equalled the course record established by Lloyd Mangrum in 1940. Player began the final day seven strokes behind but he birdied seven of the last ten holes to win by one stroke from Hubert Green, Rod Funseth and Watson.

The South African's partner that day was one Severiano Ballesteros.

Below Ben Crenshaw sinks a monster putt at the 10th in the final round in 1984.

Right With victory nearly assured, Crenshaw tees off at the 18th in the final round.

BEN CRENSHAW

'Gentle Ben' ended a 12-year professional hoodoo when he won the 1984 US Masters. 'It's a sweet, sweet thing – I don't think there will be anything sweeter for me,' he said. Crenshaw craved for a major championship – placing an intolerable burden on himself by declaring that he would die for a British Open. The Masters provided acceptable consolation. The Texan – born in Austin on 11 January 1952 – won his first start as a professional in the 1973 San Antonio-Texas Open. At his best, regarded among the finest putters in the game. In his earlier days a reckless driver, and a suspect temperament sometimes blunted his performances. But now one of the nicest guys in golf who enjoys collecting golfing artifacts.

Even so, he is more concerned with collecting golfing titles. He has won no fewer than ten times on the US PGA Tour, though even that does not reflect the true brilliance of his game. His most profitable year on the tour was in 1983, when he won the Byron Nelson Classic and pocketed 275,000 dollars for seventh place in the official money list. He also enjoyed an outstanding Ryder Cup that year at the PGA National course in Palm Beach Gardens, Florida. The Europeans were threatening to beat the Americans for the first time on their home soil. But Crenshaw gained an important point when he moved past Sandy Lyle. A combination of domestic problems and illness seemed to cause a hiccup in Crenshaw's career, following his US Masters triumph, but he used the 1986 US Open as a launching pad for better things again. Crenshaw snapped up four birdies in succession during the final round and briefly held the lead. Although he subsequently slipped back, there was no doubt that he was on his way again. 'It was tremendous getting into contention again,' said Crenshaw. 'And it was important that it should happen in a major championship. It made me feel that I had my game back together.'

Right Ben Crenshaw searching unsuccessfully for his second 'major' at the 1985 US Open, contested at Oakland Hills, Michigan.

And it was only two years later that Ballesteros, at the age of 23 years and four days, became the youngest winner of the Masters. Nicklaus had previously held that honour with his first win in 1963 when he was 23 years, two months and 16 days old.

At one stage in 1980 Ballesteros held a commanding ten-stroke lead during the final round. He faltered towards the close but he still won by four from Gibby Gilbert and Jack Newton. Three years later Ballesteros erupted at the start of the final round with such brilliance that his American rivals like Tom Kite were compelled to confess: 'It was like chasing a Ferrari in a beat-up Chevrolet.'

When Ben Crenshaw won in 1984 the entire golfing world felt relieved. Crenshaw's marvellous

Below Crenshaw about to tee off at the 12th in the 1984 final round. The hole, known as 'Golden Bell', is 155 yards with a par of three.

attitude had earned him the respect of all concerned but so far he had failed to fulfil his lifetime ambition of winning a major championship. So when he finally earned the right to enter the champion's locker, an upstairs sanctuary in the clubhouse reserved exclusively for winners of the Masters, it provided him with as much joy as it did to his friends and fans.

What it also meant was that the Masters remained in America. Yet what happened in 1985 at Augusta, as Langer clawed his way to the championship, provided further evidence that golf's stars and stripes flag is no longer flying head and shoulders above the others. The entire nation was staggered that the son of a bricklayer from West Germany had beaten the cream of American golf. Langer told them, through the columns of hundreds of newspapers from Alaska to Georgia and from California to Florida, that: 'I didn't

even know who Nicklaus and Palmer were until 1972. And when I told my friends that I wanted to become a professional golfer they told me I was mad '

In fact the Langer story is quite astonishing. His father, Erwin, as one of the millions of refugees from Sudetenland – a slice of present-day Czechoslovakia – was caught by the Russians and put on a train which, presumably, was heading for Siberia. Bernhard explains: 'My father jumped the train. He was shot at . . . but he escaped then walked all the way to Germany.' Erwin arrived in the hamlet of Anheusen where he married a local girl. He pursued his trade and worked hard for a living but Bernhard, in order to have any pocket money, had to earn his own, and this he did by caddying at the Augsberg Golf Club some five miles from his home. Bernhard's big break came when he was offered a three-year apprenticeship at the

BERNHARD LANGER

There can be no doubt that in 1985 Langer climbed the final step of the ladder to stardom. Bernhard, at the age of 27, grabbed US Masters glory when he beat off the challenge of Seve Ballesteros. It was a marvellous success for the West German and he came out first again seven days later when he won the Sea Pines Heritage Classic – his first PGA Tour win. In fact, he enjoyed a thoroughly outstanding 1985 as he took the Australian Masters and the Million Dollars Classic in South Africa, and in between won the Lufthansa German Open and the Panasonic European Open. Yet 13 years earlier he knew little about the game. Langer recalls: 'I had read a couple of magazine articles on Palmer and Nicklaus but I knew nothing else about the game.' The problem was that golf was regarded as a pastime exclusively reserved for the wealthy in Langer's homeland. So when he declared, after walking some five miles from the village in which he lived to the nearest golf club, that he planned a career in golf there were many who laughed at him.

He made significant progress as an amateur, later benefiting from the instruction he received from Heinz Fehring at Munich where he became an assistant, and he first played on the European tour in 1976. But his meteoric rise was threatened by golf's dreaded disease, the yips, and as he missed putt after putt so some of his European rivals were compelled to turn their heads and shake them in disbelief. It did seem that he would never rid himself of the twitch, but when he followed a victory in the Under-25 championship in 1979 by winning the Dunlop Masters in 1980 there was no question that he was on his way again. As a powerful driver of the ball and a magnificent long-iron player he was destined to become the greatest golfer in West German history once he had conquered the yips. Born on 27 August 1957, in Anheusen, Bavaria, he married an American wife, Vikki, and played a vital role in Europe's capture of the Ryder Cup in 1985.

Below Bernhard Langer has grown in confidence on the greens of the world.

Munich Golf Club where one of the members, following Langer's success in the German national championship, offered to sponsor him on the European tour.

The world was now Langer's oyster. But there are some bad oysters and the one that stuck in his gullet was an attack of golf's dreaded disease known as the 'yips'. To put it bluntly, Bernhard Langer could not putt. In an international event he was asked to hole putts of 12 inches by rivals who knew that he would miss. One professional even told him: 'Look, do yourself a favour and go home and become a bricklayer like your father.'

Langer, however, is made of sterner stuff than that. He said: 'I might not look it all the time but I am a very determined person. I knew that I had the game from tee to green to do well so I realized that if I could become a decent putter then my career would turn around.' Yet even when Langer started winning on the European tour, with the British Masters his first big success in 1980, there were those observers who still maintained that he could not possibly break through on the American scene where the fast greens provided problems for even the finest putters. And to think about winning Augusta was absolutely ridiculous!

Yet, putting in the unorthodox manner of having his right hand above his left when gripping the implement, Langer coaxed home putt after putt to emerge as the champion in 1985. In all the fairytale stories of Augusta there seemed no reason to believe that there would one to better this . . . but then who could have predicted that Jack Nicklaus, at the age of 46 years and 82 days, would in 1986 become the oldest winner in the history of the US Masters?

Right Langer coaxed home putt after putt in 1985 to emerge as US Masters champion – though he lost the title in 1986 to Jack Nicklaus.

IN THE BAG

What's in a bag? Nick Faldo shows that the game of golf involves more equipment than just clubs, balls and tees. You have to be prepared for all kinds of weather – so waterproofs and mittens are a must – and with the likelihood of being out on the course for approaching five hours it is sensible to take along some fruit as nourishment. Here Nick shows everything that he takes out with him . . . and why the caddies sometimes show the strain!

FALDO ON SHORT-IRON GOLF

Most amateurs seem dumbfounded when they miss a green with anything between an 8-iron and a wedge. They seem almost inconsolable if, having decided that the shot in question requires a 9-iron, the ball comes up short of the green.

The answer is simple. Most amateurs do not take enough care and attention with these clubs. They seem to think that they are the easiest clubs in the bag to play. Well, that might be the case but I cannot impress enough how much there is to learn about these clubs.

What you must set out to do is to learn your limitations with the short clubs. It is no good walking up to a ball and blasting it with a 9-iron. You must know the maximum and minimum distances you can hit the ball with that club. So take the time to go down to the practice range and pace out a stretch up to 150 yards. Put markers on the ground from, say, 80 yards onwards, and then experiment with each club. A lot of amateurs kid themselves how far they can strike with an 8- or a 9-iron – by experimenting with these clubs I expect most people to be surprised.

It is really quite easy to understand. I have played with very few amateurs who hit the ball past the stick. Mostly their shots come up short. The reason is that they seem intent on believing that they are gorillas, with every club from the driver down, so they pull out an 8-iron, or even a 9, when they should be thinking in terms of a 7.

More importantly, by taking one club more you will give yourself the opportunity of making a nice, smooth swing instead of trying to crash the ball on to the green. And, by knowing that you have learned the range of your shots with each iron, you can now concentrate on shaping the shot so that the ball reacts in the required manner when it lands on the green.

As a guide, I hit with a sand wedge from anything up to 90 yards, with an absolute maximum of 95 yards; with a pitching wedge from between 90 and 120 yards; with a 9-iron from 120 to 130 yards; and with an 8-iron from 130 to 140 yards. Conditions, of course, can affect the distances covered, since a ball will fly further in warm air or it can be buffeted by a wind, but if you have taken care to learn the limitations of each of your clubs then I believe you will make significant progress in this area.

Right Be bold and get the ball up to the hole so that you give yourself a fair chance of holing out with your next shot.

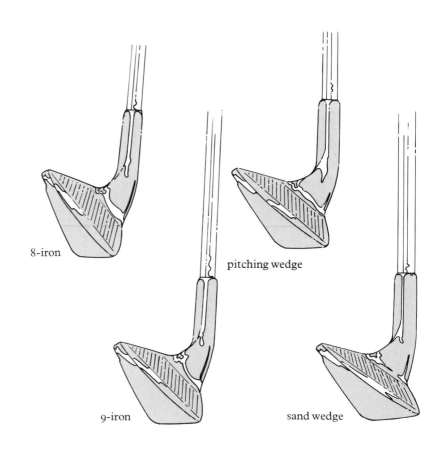

8-iron

pitching wedge

9-iron

sand wedge

CHAPTER THREE
THE AMERICAN DREAM

CHAPTER THREE

THE AMERICAN DREAM –

the US Open Championship

Just how little muscle American golf authorities had in 1895 can be measured by the ease with which they succumbed to demands that the US Amateur Championship be pushed back a few weeks. It had been originally scheduled to take place in Newport, Rhode Island, at the time of the established America's Cup yacht races. But the sailing boys were not prepared to have their occasion running alongside a sport so new to the country that it was not even part of the American way of life.

Who could argue? In the America's Cup *Defender*, the US

entry, beat England's *Valkyrie III* 3-0. In the first US Open, a few weeks later, Horace Rawlins, a 21-year-old Englishman, won the title with the Scottish professional Willie Dunn taking second place. Names to conjure with? Not quite, unless you are an historian of the game. But over the next few years, until 1911 to be precise, the Americans were compelled to regard each US Open as an education as British golfers dominated the championship.

The US Open had come into being as something of an afterthought. The United States Golf Association, formed in December 1894, was above all concerned with running praiseworthy US Amateur Championships following complaints that previous events had been organized under the wrong format and at clubs incapable of conducting national championships.

So after Charles Blair Macdonald, coincidentally the leading critic, had won the Amateur title in 1895 the professionals were invited to play for the Open Championship. It was hardly surprising that from the moment Rawlins won the 150 dollars first prize and a 50-dollar gold medal the British players dominated the scene.

To the Americans, hitting a little white ball from one point to another, with the intention of getting it in a hole little larger than a tin can, was about as foreign as

the thought of being beaten at anything. So it was rather hard for them to accept the annual US Open results as James Foulis, a Scot, won in 1896 followed by Joe Lloyd, Fred Herd and Willie Smith. Then, in 1900, the great Harry Vardon, who had arrived with J. H. Taylor in the United States for a series of exhibitions, stopped off in Chicago at the time of the US Open. Vardon won and Taylor came second but the Americans, fast catching the bug, now began to appreciate the skills of these golfing craftsmen.

It was Willie Anderson's turn the following year. In fact he won the US Open four times in five attempts, broken only by the victory of Laurie Auchterlonie in 1902. Anderson, a dour Scot who shunned publicity, was educated in North Berwick. Every man, woman and child played golf in North Berwick at the time when Anderson was born there in the late 1870s, so when the best of the British golfers went over to America it was easy to understand why initially they dominated the scene. It was the likes of Anderson who spread the gospel.

The professionals also owe one very important debt to Anderson. It was he who first made sure that they were accorded some status. In 1901, at the start of the first US Open he was to win, an officer of the Myopia Hunt Club in Hamilton, Massachusetts, made the high and mighty announcement that the amateurs would eat in the

Previous spread America's 'big two' – Tom Watson (left) and Jack Nicklaus – battle it out.

Above J. H. Taylor (right), five-times winner of the British Open, never won the US Open.

dining room and the professionals would eat in the kitchen. Anderson lost his usual reticence and raged: 'Na, na . . . we're na goin' t' eat in the kitchen.' As a result a special tent was erected for the professionals and that was the start of their climb up the social ladder.

Sadly, Anderson died young in 1910. The death certificate stated that he died of arteriosclerosis – hardening of the arteries – but others have put forward the theory that it was as a result of acute alcoholism. Whatever the true reason, he was unquestionably the first player to dominate the US Open. His record of four wins still stands, although Bobby Jones, Ben Hogan and Jack Nicklaus have all equalled it. It is the kind of company which, on paper, reflects the enormous talent that Anderson must have possessed although, unfortunately, there is not enough information to suggest precisely how he would have fared in another era. It has been claimed, by other professionals who knew him, that he would have held his own even with the likes of the formidable Jones.

It is certainly worth bearing in mind that whereas the modern-day professional is allowed to carry 14 clubs in his bag under the rules of golf, Anderson chose to take only eight. The names by which he knew them were a driver, a brassie, a cleek, a mid-iron, a mashie, a large mashie-niblick, a pitching iron and a putting cleek. In today's terms – a driver, a 2-wood, a 1-iron, a 3-iron, a 5-iron, an 8-iron with an oversized blade, a 9-iron and a highly lofted blade putter.

Right Jack Nicklaus is one of only four players who have each won the US Open a record four times. Well spaced out, Nicklaus's victories occurred in 1962, 1967, 1972 and 1980.

Anderson's departure from this world came before the British dominance of the US Open was ended. But it was threatened in 1910 by a cocky youngster from Philadelphia called Johnny McDermott. He was eighteen years old, came from the ranks of the caddies, and he arrived on the scene with the one intention of letting the British competitors know, in no uncertain terms, that he regarded it a downright liberty that they should have exclusivity on what should be a part of America's sporting heritage. He had to be

content with second place in 1910 but he did become the first homebred champion in 1911 and, furthermore, he successfully defended the title the following year.

McDermott's triumphs sparked a dramatic U-turn in America's golfing fortune. The game was now becoming as popular as apple pie and the nation begrudged giving a piece of the action to any overseas player who 'trespassed' on their fairways. Britain's Ted Ray did win in 1920 but it was not until South Africa's Gary Player won in 1965

Ouimet, out in 43 strokes on the last day, had taken five at the short tenth when Vardon and Ray posted their 72-hole aggregates of 304. Ouimet would have to play the last eight in one under fours to force a play-off at The Country Club, Brookline, in his home state. He achieved it by hitting with a jigger, a shallow-faced iron that has the loft of a 4-iron, to 20 feet at the 17th. The putt went in for a birdie and a five-footer for a par at the last sent Ouimet into an 18-hole play-off with the great Vardon and Ray.

The story goes that Ray soon fell behind so that Vardon was left to contend with the unflappable

Ouimet and for the first time in his career Vardon was seen to light a cigarette on the golf course. If he did then, like the match he struck, Vardon's flame flickered and died as Ouimet chastised the two Britons. He scored 72, Vardon took 77 and Ray 78.

So the US Open truly became American. Some marvellous players now have their names engraved on the trophy, including Gene Sarazen, Byron Nelson, Cary Middlecoff, Billy Casper, Arnold Palmer, Gene Littler and Lee Trevino who, in winning in 1968, enjoyed the first success of his career on the US Tour.

Above Gary Player's win in 1965 was the first by an overseas player since Britain's Ted Ray in 1920.

Right Lee Trevino, who won the US Open in 1968 and 1971. Nicklaus was runner-up both times.

that the US Open went overseas again.

What stirred American interest more than McDermott's successive wins was the victory of Francis Ouimet in 1913. Ouimet had graduated from playing with his brothers on some rough holes carved in the back yard of their Boston home to becoming, at the age of 20, a semi-finalist in the US Amateur Championship. More importantly he had plenty of ambition and he wanted to play in the US Open.

So a raw amateur was taking on the professionals including Vardon and Ray. Vardon, already a five-times winner of the British Open, and Ray, the reigning British Open champion, against . . . the Massachusetts amateur champion. There were others, of course, but all eyes were on these three players.

GENE SARAZEN

Maker of the first shot 'heard around the world' and the most famous shot in golf. It came in the 1935 US Masters at Augusta when he struck a 3-wood at the 15th and the ball disappeared into the hole for an albatross two. He went into a 36-hole play-off with the luckless Craig Wood and won. Holed another beauty in the 1973 US Open at Troon when he aced the eighth hole, known as the Postage Stamp, then casually walked on to the green and put his hat over the hole. 'I wanted the ball to stay there,' he joked. Born Harrison, New York, on 27 February 1902, he won the British Open in 1932 and became one of the few players to win that championship and the US Open in the same year. He had previously won the US Open in 1922.

Below Gene Sarazen.   **Right** Billy Casper.

BILLY CASPER

Followed Arnold Palmer into the record books when, in 1970, he became only the second player to pass the one million dollar mark in earnings on the official US PGA Tour. Born 24 June 1931, he launched his career with a 1956 victory in the Labatt tournament.

Totalled 51 victories on the PGA Tour, including 1959 and 1966 US Opens and 1970 US Masters, before switching to the Seniors Tour. A Mormon, he has 11 children and six grandchildren and his special interests include church work and fishing. Often wears knickerbockers and uses specially tailored hickory-shafted clubs.

Even so, the three names that have dominated the championship are Jones, Hogan and Nicklaus. Jones won in 1923, 1926, 1929 and 1930. The American dream, of course, had died in 1929 with the US Stock Market Crash on Black Friday, 29 October. It is the feeling of some golf observers that Jones's dream, which was destined to become a reality, almost died that year as well. He had four shots to spare with four holes to play then took seven at the par four 15th and three-putted the next. He put his approach to the last in the rough and chipped to 12 feet – a putt he required to force a play-off with Al Espinosa. Jones made it, and won the play-off, and there are those who believe that if he had lost then he would not have completed the historic Grand Slam of winning four major championships in 1930.

The US Open continued through the Depression years to the Second World War. There were some marvellous performances, but none better than that of Sarazen in 1932 at Fresh Meadows in Flushing, New York. In those days the last 36 holes were packed into the final day. Sarazen, seven behind and standing on the ninth tee in the morning, decided uncharacteristically that it was time to throw caution to the winds. He attacked everything – covering the back nine in 32 for a 70. In the afternoon he swept to the turn in 32 and came home in 34 for a 66. He had covered the last 28 holes in 100 strokes and he had won the US Open again ten years after his first triumph.

It is players like Sarazen who, of course, have created the love affair with golf in which millions of people around the world are involved. But few will deny that it has become increasingly popular since being discovered by television. It was at St Louis in 1947 that television first captured the US Open: a camera behind the 18th green transmitted a picture so that 600 homes in St Louis were able to see Lew Worsham tie with Sam Snead before winning in a play-off.

In 1948 Hogan won the US Open, and six other events, and the curtain had risen on a new era. Cruelly, however, it was to be horrifyingly interrupted. Hogan left the Riviera Country Club in Los Angeles in a state of exhaustion intending to drive to his home in Fort Worth, Texas. He climbed into his Cadillac, with his wife Valerie alongside him, and said: 'I must go home. It is time to rest. I want to die an old man, not a young one.'

How prophetic words can threaten to be. That night, in thick fog, Hogan drove slowly into a small town called Van Horn. Within seconds of seeing two headlamps emerging from the mist towards his car there was a sickening crash. Hogan had time to fling his body over his wife in a loving attempt to protect her. In fact he probably saved his own life at the same time because after the crash the steering-wheel column was found to have pierced the driver's seat like a spear.

But Hogan still suffered. He had a double fracture of the pelvis. He had broken his left ankle, his collar-bone and goodness knows how many ribs. And his left knee was badly damaged. He was to be on his back for two months during which time there was further emergency treatment for blood clots. The question was whether Hogan would ever walk again

Left Sam Snead took part in the first Open to be televised – at St Louis in 1947. Lew Worsham beat Snead.

MANUEL PINERO

Manuel Pinero has one of those sad, soft Spanish faces that makes the ladies want to mother the little man from Madrid. It is, however, an illusion. Pinero is a gentle man but beneath the 'cuddly' exterior he is as hard an opponent as can be found in the world of professional golf. Only one golfer prevents Pinero from being the outstanding Spanish player of his generation, one Severiano Ballesteros, and it was the inspired combination of the two of them that, in reality, clinched Ryder Cup victory for Europe in 1985. Together they defeated Curtis Strange and Mark O'Meara, Andy North and Peter Jacobsen, Craig Stadler and Hal Sutton. Then, when it came to the last day singles at The Belfry, Pinero got his wish when he was first man out for the European side, pitted against Lanny Wadkins, the hard-man of the American side and their biggest banker for victory in those few, heart-tugging hours. When Pinero defeated Wadkins 3 and 1, the news spread back through the European team like a tidal wave of confidence and Tony Jacklin openly embraced his little amigo in front of thousands of spectators.

Yet if that was one of the happiest moments of Pinero's career, one of the saddest came in June 1986 when – again in front of spectators and a huge television audience – he took an illegal stance in the rough during the second round of the Dunhill British Masters at Woburn. The evidence on film was condemning, Pinero's explanation extraordinary for someone who has been a pro since 1968. 'I did not realize I was breaking the rule. I thought I could do what I did. I've done it in the past and would have done it again in the future,' he said after being expelled from the tournament. It is a mark of the high respect for Pinero that the majority of fellow players accept that explanation. Born the son of a pig farmer in September 1952, Pinero moved to Madrid when 11 years old and learned his golf as caddy at the Club de Campo where he worked six days a week alongside José-María Cañizares and Antonio Garrido. He has won nine tournaments in Europe plus individual and team World Cup victories.

Left Manuel Pinero teamed up with Seve Ballesteros to bolster Europe's 1985 Ryder Cup team, then beat Lanny Wadkins 3 and 1 on his own.

rather than whether he would ever golf again.

That he achieved both, and went on to win four US Opens as well as two US Masters, two US PGA Championships and one British Open, is a measure of the man they called 'Bantam Ben' on account of his light build. From his earliest years he had been prepared to turn his hand to anything to earn enough money to finance his golf. He worked in banks, garages, hotels and even in the oilfields. In spite of those hard times Ben Hogan remains, to those who witnessed his golf at the time, the man who played for the glory.

And what glory there was in 1953! He won the US Masters and, by the time he had also won the US Open, Hogan had decided, at the age of 40, to make what was to be his one and only attempt to win the British Open. Hogan must have had misgivings when he first arrived at Carnoustie for he described the greens as being mowed once a week, maybe, and the fairways once a month. As for the bunkers: he put them down to being placed as if by a man

throwing rice at a wedding. Hogan went into the rough only once off the tee throughout the 108 holes which included the 36-hole qualifying examination, and he triumphed. He had proved himself to be the best in the world; even so, he had won his last major championship.

Hogan's retirement in 1957 left a void in the game. But it was about to be filled by Arnold Palmer, who won the US Open in 1960, and then by Jack Nicklaus. Whereas Palmer won only once, Nicklaus won in 1962, 1967, 1972 and 1980. Thus he equalled the four victories

of Anderson, Jones, and Hogan.

There were other notable wins like that by Orville Moody, who putted cross-handed to win in 1969, and the one by Ken Venturi who in 1964 survived both local and sectional qualifying rounds before winning at the Congressional Country Club in Washington.

Yet if you have British blood running through your veins there is nothing to compare with the events of 1970. Tony Jacklin, who had won the British Open eleven months earlier, at last rekindled memories of the early days of the US Open – when British players reigned supreme – by winning at the Hazeltine National club at Chaska, Minneapolis. There was, quite simply, nobody to touch Jacklin that week as he won by seven shots from Dave Hill. Jacklin had won the British and US Opens and he was still only 26. Palmer, on the other hand, had not won his first major championship until he was 27. The tragedy, as far as Jacklin is concerned, is that he did not win another 'major' in his playing career.

So, once more, Britain was looking for a player to take on the Americans on their home soil. Sandy Lyle attempted to follow in the footsteps of Jacklin by collecting the 1986 US Open at Shinnecock Hills as a follow up to his British Open victory. But it was not to be. In fact it turned out to be the Australians who posed the greatest 'overseas' challenge as the 1980s unfolded. David Graham won at Merion in 1981 and, at Winged Foot in 1984, Greg Norman took Zoeller to a play-off which the latter won.

Norman made another inspirational charge for the 1986 title. Moving into the final round he was leading but then fell away as

Above right Ben Hogan, four-times winner of the Open. He is seen here competing for the Canada (later World) cup at Wentworth in 1956.

Right Greg Norman sinks a 40-foot putt at the last hole of the 1984 Open at Winged Foot.

DAVID GRAHAM

Started golfing at the age of 14 when he found a set of left-handed clubs in his garage in Windsor, Australia. Two years later, apprenticed to a golf shop in Melbourne, he switched to a right-handed set. Enjoyed success in Europe, the Far East and his native Australia before moving to live in America. At his best on tough, uncompromising courses such as that at Merion in 1981 when he shot a last-round 67 to win the US Open. Bill Rogers, former British Open champion, remarked: 'He hit 18 greens in regulation and in the last round of the US Open that is unbelievable.' Scored his first US win in the 1972 Cleveland Open and he also won the US PGA Championship in 1979. Born 23 May 1946, his interests include designing golf clubs.

What is remarkable about the Australian is the number of times when he has been compelled to play 'head-down' golf in order to extract victory when defeat seemed more likely. There was the time in the 1979 US PGA Championship, when he was cruising to victory and then double-bogied the 18th hole enabling Ben Crenshaw to tie with him. In such circumstances it is inevitable that the other player will have the advantage but Graham showed what a gutsy player he is by rolling in a tremendous birdie putt at the third extra hole to take the title. And in his first victory on the American tour in 1972 – the Cleveland Open – he had to beat his close friend Bruce Devlin in a play-off. In fact, he had teamed up with Devlin to win the World Cup for Australia in 1970 and he enhanced his reputation as a fine team member by assisting Graham Marsh and Greg Norman to an Australian victory in the Dunhill Cup at St Andrews in 1985. As an individual he has enjoyed many fine triumphs around the world, which include winning the World Match-Play Championship at Wentworth in 1976, the Chunichi Crowns in Japan the same year, and the Lancôme Trophy in France in 1981 and 1982.

Below David Graham wins the Open at Merion in 1981. Once he had taken over the lead from George Burns at the 14th, he didn't look back.

START	LEADERS	PAR	1	2	3	4	5	6	7	8	9	10	11	12	13	14	15	16	17	18	MESSAGES
			4	5	3	5	4	4	4	4	3	4	4	4	3	4	4	4	3	4	
7	BURNS		7	7	7	6	6	6	6	6	6	5	5	5	5	5	4	5			
4	GRAHAM D		5	6	6	6	5	5	5	5	5	5	5	5	6	7	7	7			
3	ROGERS		3	3	3	3	3	2	2	3	4	3	4	4	4	4	3	3	4		
2	RODRIGUEZ		2	2	2	3	2	1	0	1	1	1	0	1	0	0	0	1	0	0	
1	THORPE		1	1	1	1	0	0	0	1	1	2	2	2	2	2	1	0	1		
2	NICKLAUS		2	2	1	1	2	2	2	2	3	3	2	2	2	2	2	1	0		
1	CRENSHAW		2	2	2	2	2	2	1	1	2			0	0	0	1				
	CONNER		1	0	0	0															
	COOK J																				
2	SCHROEDER																				

GREG NORMAN

Nicknamed the 'Great White Shark' for his tumbling blond hair – often bleached white by the sun – and his birthplace, Queensland's Gold Coast, where he hunted the fearsome beasts, Greg Norman didn't begin playing the game until he was 16 after caddieing for his mother, but within two years he had reduced a 27 handicap to scratch. His ambition had been to be a pilot in the Royal Australian Air Force but he was soon leaving the world's greatest players in his slipstream after turning professional in 1976, and has been aiming for the sky ever since.

He earned a formidable reputation in Europe before joining the US circuit full-time in 1984, when he announced his arrival with victories in the Kemper and Canadian Opens. It was in the same year that he was pipped in a play-off for the US Open by Fuzzy Zoeller, but what he lost in prestige he gained in popularity with the 18-hole decider rated one of the most sporting in the long history of the Championship. He went desperately close to winning a major again in 1986 when presented with a great chance to tie with Jack Nicklaus for the US Masters. But he pushed his approach to the right of the 18th green at Augusta and the chance was gone. It led to a chorus of 'choker' but

Norman – born on 10 February 1955 – possesses a frightening determined streak and his talent was rewarded when he won the Open Championship by five shots at Turnberry three months later.

His ability is based on an awesome power, particularly from the tee, and his prodigious drives have helped the son of a mining engineer to nearly 40 victories around the world. Greg is now based at Bay Hill, Florida, with his wife Laura and children Morgan-Leigh and Gregory. He owes much of his meteoric rise to Jack Nicklaus, whose books Golf My Way and 55 Ways to Play Golf taught him the basics of a game he is sure to grace for many years to come.

Right Greg Norman – a great sportsman, a great showman and, finally, a great champion. He deserved his win.

Raymond Floyd, at the age of 43 years and nine months, became the oldest winner in the history of the Championship. But it is the Zoeller-Norman confrontation that will live long in the memory of those who witnessed the last hole. Norman, playing one match ahead of Zoeller, had missed the green to the right. He was given a free drop because his ball was near to a spectator stand and from there he pitched the ball past the flag so that it came to rest just off the green. When the curling 40-foot putt disappeared into the hole Zoeller was standing in the middle of the 18th fairway. He believed that Norman had holed for a birdie and, in one gigantic act of sportsmanship, took his white towel from his bag and waved it in mock surrender.

It was the kind of touching moment which brings a sport to life. Too often today sport is regarded as being about dollars and pounds. To Zoeller, and Norman, that moment was about glory. That the play-off unfolded in such sporting circumstances only served to underline that not every professional is constantly and selfishly concerned with making money. The spectators paid to see the Championship contested and Zoeller and Norman gave them true value for their money.

Even so, as far as American golf is concerned, Nicklaus and Watson have been the dominant players in recent times. And in 1982 they combined to produce one of the most exciting finishes as Nicklaus came through the field with a closing 69 at Pebble Beach – to many golfers the eighth wonder of the world – in California. As Nicklaus signed his card, Watson arrived at the 17th tee. Watson would need to birdie one of the last two holes to win; Nicklaus felt the prospect of being bathed in glory again.

He must have felt all the more confident when Watson's tee shot at the par three 17th left the ball in a collar of grass between two bunkers. Nicklaus began thinking in terms of a fifth US Open – one more than Anderson, Jones and Hogan. Watson was in ankle-deep rough some 18 feet from the hole. He had no more than 12 feet of the green between him and the ball and the green ran downhill away from him. It seemed a reasonable bet that he would finish 20, maybe 25, feet past the flag. A three would be miracle, a four more likely.

Bruce, Watson's caddie, said: 'Get it close, Tom.' Watson, studying the shot, looked across and smiled: 'I'm not going to get it close, I'm going to make it.'

Right Jack Nicklaus clasps the Open trophy for the fourth time – here at Baltusrol, New Jersey, in 1980.

FUZZY ZOELLER

Frank Urban Zoeller, known to the world of golf as Fuzzy, certainly calls into question the claim that the American circuit lacks a character. He constantly whistles while he works, his permanent grin and his endless wisecracking cloaking severe back pains which put him in hospital for a week on the opening day of the 1984 US PGA Championship. A few weeks earlier he had won the US Open at Winged Foot – a victory immortalized by an astonishing display of sportsmanship by Zoeller. He was convinced that Greg Norman had sunk a 40ft birdie putt on the 18th green for the title and, standing on the same fairway, waved a white towel in mock surrender. It was only when Zoeller reached the putting surface that he realized it was for par and he tied with the Australian before winning the play-off by the crushing margin of 67 to 75. A month later he was back in hospital, this time needing surgery on ruptured discs – a legacy of his basketball prowess at High School.

Zoeller, born in New Albany, Indiana, in November 1951, first hit the headlines in the 1976 Quad Cities Open when he birdied the last eight holes of his first round to equal the 1961 record of Bob Goalby. But he blossomed as a superstar three years later, when he won the Andy Williams San Diego Open and the US Masters at his first attempt. That feat had been achieved only once before – by Horton Smith in 1934! And he won it the hard way, beginning the final round six shots adrift of Ed Snead and then defeating Snead and Tom Watson at the second hole of a sudden-death play-off. Even Zoeller does not know if his back will allow him to continue his professional career. But if he is forced to retire he will not be the only loser – the galleries of the world would lose a man renowned as much for his humour as for his tremendous talent.

Left Victory in the 1984 US Open confirmed Fuzzy Zoeller's status among the game's superstars.

Watson bumped the leading edge of his sand iron under the ball and the ball popped up and landed on the green. Watson yelled: 'That's in!' And, sure enough, the ball dropped for a birdie two.

Nicklaus knew he was beaten. Bill Rogers, who was partnering Watson, later said: 'Tom could have hit that shot a hundred times and never got the ball close.' Nicklaus butted in: 'Make that one thousand times.'

Watson, however, insisted later: 'I've practised that shot for hours, days, months. The grass around the greens at the US Open is always like that so you must be confident of getting up and down in a maximum of two if you are to keep your score intact.'

It is a real example to us all that practice makes perfect.

Right At the 1982 Open at Pebble Beach, Tom Watson achieved an astonishing birdie two at the 17th in the final round to win against Jack Nicklaus.

Below The dramatic setting of the 7th green at Pebble Beach, California.

ANDY NORTH

Won his third US tour event – and his second US Open! – when successful at Oakland Hills, Birmingham, Michigan, in 1985. Many thought his first US Open triumph in 1978 was a fluke – 'I don't go along with that,' says North – but he produced a great shot to secure the title in 1985 with a bunker escape to a few inches at the penultimate hole. An elbow injury threatened his career but two years after surgery he completed a tremendous comeback. Born Thorp, Wisconsin, on 9 March 1950, he stands 6ft 4in tall. Enjoys coaching football when not playing golf.

Yet it was an unusual ailment which assisted North's entry into golf. At school it was discovered that a bone in his knee had stopped growing and was disintegrating. He spent no less than 18 months on crutches and during that time he was ordered to give up his beloved football – and basketball – but was informed that he could play golf if he chose. The reason? In America you can ride in a cart! North's father was a low-handicap golfer and, as he was no stranger to the game, North decided that he should try and improve. He won the Wisconsin high school championship in 1966 and 1967, the State Amateur in 1969 and, after entering the University of Florida, he was chosen All-American for three years and won the prestigious Western Amateur in 1971. He turned professional in 1972 and made gradual progress on the US PGA Tour – climbing from 64th in 1973 to 14th in 1978, when he won the first of those two US Opens. It was an anxious affair for North at Cherry Hills, because he led by four strokes with five to play, but came to the last needing a bogey to win . . . which is what he made! He was bunkered in three but, as he was to do again in 1985, he produced a superb recovery and then holed from four feet to take the title. The waiting was over.*

Below Andy North triumphs in the 1985 US Open. He beat runners-up Dave Barr, T. C. Chen and Dennis Watson by one stroke.

ANDY BEAN

At 6ft 4ins and 220 lbs, Andy Bean has the build and the reputation of a heavyweight boxer. At one time he was more famous for wrestling with an alligator – he did it once in Florida as a stunt – and for biting golf balls in half (his dentist persuaded him to give up that hobby), than for his ability as a golfer. Gradually, however, the big man made a name for himself as a player not only of power but of finesse also and for the last 10 years he has been one of the biggest names in the American game and therefore one of the biggest in the world. Nine tournament wins in that time have taken him over the 2 million dollar money mark and gained Bean entry into one of the most exclusive clubs in sport. Yet he – and many experts – remain confused that he has not stamped even more authority on a game he sometimes finds almost too easy. 'It would be nice to win one of the majors, but I can't really complain. Maybe my day will come, maybe it won't,' he says. It is exactly the sort of laid-back remark one would expect Bean to deliver. Like many 'gentle giants' he is easy-going to the point of falling down! Little, if anything, appears to bother his slow amble through life. Except, that is, for the constant and irritating variety of injuries and illness that seem to snap at his heels like a particularly annoying, yelping dog. The worst injury was when he fractured his wrist in 1981. The legacy of that is a constant pain in the wrist when playing golf, which sometimes radically affects his ability to deliver all his awesome power to the ball. From the ball's point of view, at least, that is a merciful release . . .

Right Andy Bean, one of the most prodigious drivers in the game.

FALDO ON ESCAPE SHOTS

Some observers called Tom Watson lucky when he chipped in from ankle-deep rough for a birdie two at the penultimate hole to ensure success in the 1982 United States Open Championship. But I didn't call it lucky. It was, quite simply, a gem of a shot.

Consider the facts. Watson, tied in front with Jack Nicklaus, knew that most spectators were convinced he was about to take four and lose the championship. His ball was in the high rough, skirting the green at the 209-yard 17th hole at Pebble Beach, California, and he faced a shot of 18 feet from some six feet off the green. His caddie urged him to get his ball close to the hole.

Watson, however, had other ideas: he was determined to make it.

Now the way that Watson played that shot is a salutary lesson to us all. He was confident. He knew that the ball was sitting up sufficiently for him to get the leading edge of his sand iron under it. And, after 'feeling' the shot in his mind, he took one last look and he swung that sand wedge softly. The ball popped out, just as he had expected, and the moment it touched the green Watson knew that it would go in.

It was an education for us all. To begin with Watson used a sand wedge – and, make no mistake, that is the only club to employ for such shots. Too many amateurs regard the sand wedge as a club simply for using in bunkers. That it most certainly is not: it is a very important club. Watson's action, too, was spot-on. You must strike the ball with an easy descending blow so that it pops up. It's what I term a 'chunk' shot – a short, sharp stroke to be played with as positive an attitude as possible.

The easiest way to learn to play the shot is to get your weight forward on the leading foot then pick up the club slightly with the right hand – vice versa if you are a 'leftie' – and chop down and through the ball. You will not get the ball to stop quickly on a green from out of thick grass so you must allow for a lot of run. Practice makes perfect – and you only have to ask Tom Watson to know that.

Left Watson's magnificent chip shot out of rough during the 1982 US Open at Pebble Beach, California.

Right Nick Faldo executes a smart recovery from the undergrowth.

SOME TOP CONTESTANTS FROM AROUND THE WORLD

Ian Baker-Finch *Learned the game with the help of tuition from five-times Open champion Peter Thomson. He won the 1983 New Zealand Open, four years after turning professional, then led the Open Championship at St Andrews in 1984. But he crashed out of the* title race with a closing 79. The Australian gained an important breakthrough with his Scandinavian Open triumph on the 1985 European circuit.

Fred Couples *Victory in the Tournament Players' Championship* at Ponte Vedra, Florida, in 1984 stamped Couples as a player with potential. This powerful striker, who strikes his drives on average 276 yards out, has been assisted by working with former US Masters champion Gay Brewer. He birdied each of the last six holes in the 1982 US PGA Championship to finish joint third.

Rodger Davis *The dapper Australian, who dresses in plus-twos and matching sweaters and long socks, gained his finest success when he won the Whyte and Mackay PGA Championship at Wentworth in 1986. He has campaigned regularly on the European circuit and also won the State Express Classic at The Belfry in 1981.*

David Frost *Followed in the footsteps of compatriot Gary Player by winning on his native South African circuit (Gordon's Gin Classic, 1983) then in Europe (Cannes Open, 1984) before turning to the United States. Of course, he has a long, long way to go to emulate Player's achievements but he was runner-up in the Houston Open in 1985.*

Jay Haas *His uncle is former US Masters champion Bob Goalby. A highly rated golfer, who regularly challenges for titles, he has enjoyed*

Left Australian Ian Baker-Finch stumbled after leading the Open

several victories including the Hall of Fame Classic in 1982. He was in the 1975 US Walker Cup team and the 1983 Ryder Cup team.

Donnie Hammond *From the moment he won the US PGA Tour qualifying school by an astounding 14 shots there seemed little doubt that this young American from Frederick, Maryland, would make the grade. He proved the point in 1986 by taking the Bob Hope Chrysler Classic title in Palm Springs, California.*

Scott Hoch *A member of the Walker Cup team in 1979, when he also finished runner-up in the Amateur Championship, he has won several tournaments, including the Casio World Open in Japan in 1982, but is constantly troubled by a bad back.*

Peter Jacobsen *He is in tremendous demand for clinics and exhibitions as he can give entertaining imitations of the game's superstars. Jacobsen, a member of the 1985 US Ryder Cup team, is also a fine player himself. He has proved that by winning not only on his own circuit but also in the Johnnie Walker Trophy in Madrid (twice) and in the 1979 Western Australian Open. He comes from Portland, Oregon.*

Wayne Levi *This 5ft 9in golfer from Little Falls, New York, maintained his winning form when he took his eighth US tour title by capturing the Georgia-Pacific Atlanta Classic in 1985. In 1982 at the Hawaiian Open he became the first player to win a US Tour event*

Above Peter Jacobsen shows his style with a deft approach.

with a coloured golf ball. His choice? Orange.

Roger Maltbie *The personable Californian went nine years from capturing the Memorial Tournament in 1976 to winning again on the US PGA Tour . . . but when he did, he did so in style. There was a success in the 1985 Westchester Classic, then another in the World Series of Golf at Firestone, which he won by four strokes.*

Graham Marsh *This former teacher of mathematics, from Kalgoorlie, near Perth, Australia, is the brother of former test cricket wicket-keeper Rodney Marsh. But he is far better known as a golfer, with no less than*

50 tournament wins to his credit. A regular campaigner in Europe, he won the Lawrence Batley International and KLM Dutch Open in 1985.

Mark McCumber *The Florida-based golfer, who won twice in 1983, returned to form in style when he held off the likes of Tom Kite and Jack Nicklaus to win the Doral-Eastern Open in 1985. He also keeps himself busy by designing golf courses.*

Mark McNulty *Won five times to top the South African tour Order of Merit in 1986 – the fourth time he has achieved that distinction. The Zimbabwe-born player gained victories on the European circuit in the 1979 Greater Manchester Open and the 1980 German Open.*

Larry Mize *With the birthplace of Augusta, Georgia, it would not require too much imagination to know how much Mize wants to succeed. The trouble is that although he won the Danny Thomas-Memphis Classic in 1983, he too often finds one player to edge him out on his good weeks. He finished runner-up to John Mahaffey in the Tournament Players' Championship in 1986.*

Gil Morgan *A painful shoulder injury has hindered his career although the Oklahoma-based golfer enjoyed a string of fine wins including the World Series of Golf in 1978. He was also a member of the US Ryder Cup teams in 1979 and 1983.*

Tommy Nakajima *The Japanese golfer became such a regular winner in 1985 and 1986 that he edged past Isao Aoki as the Far East player most likely to win a major championship. He will not, however, be allowed to forget his experience at the 17th 'Road' hole at St Andrews in the 1978 Open Championship when he tried, tried, tried and tried again to escape from a bunker . . . eventually marking a 13 on his card.*

Right Tommy Nakajima pushed Greg Norman most of the way during the 1986 Open Championship.

Larry Nelson *Has rightly earned the reputation for being a player who likes tough courses – winning the US PGA Championship in front of thousands of his hometown followers at the Atlanta Athletic Club in Georgia then capturing the US Open at Oakmont in 1983.*

Dan Pohl *This long hitter from Mount Pleasant, Michigan, lost a play-off for the US Masters in 1982*

to Craig Stadler. In fact he has built a number of fine tournament challenges from the time that he joined the tour in 1978. But a victory eluded him until he moved through to win the 1986 Colonial National Invitation in Fort Worth.

Nick Price *A regular competitor on the European circuit, where he won the 1980 Swiss Open, before he opted to take his talent to the US*

tour. *Born in Durban, South Africa, he emphasized that it was the correct decision by winning the World Series of Golf in 1983. He was runner-up to Tom Watson in the Open at Royal Troon in 1982 and fifth in the 1985 US PGA Championship. He also established a new record for Augusta with a 63 in the third round of the 1986 US Masters.*

Scott Simpson *The Californian confesses he surprised himself when he won the 1980 Western Open on the tough Butler National course. But he won again at the 1984 Manufacturers' Hanover Westchester Classic and he is accepted as a fine,*

consistent performer who drives the ball with tremendous precision.

Doug Tewell *He won twice in 1980 but was compelled to wait until 1986 before he moved into the winner's berth again. He did so at the Los Angeles Open. A bad back has often hindered the Louisiana man's attempts to win other titles.*

Bob Tway *A rising star in the world of American golf, as he emphasized during a tremendous 1986 campaign. After winning the Shearson Lehman and Westchester Classic tournaments, he gained success in a 'major' by coming from*

Above Nick Price, a regular contender for the major championships.

behind to pip Greg Norman for the US PGA Championship. Tway is one of the tallest of American golfers – he stands 6ft 4in.

Dennis Watson *The South African, who played for several seasons on the European circuit without much reward, has certainly made his mark on the US tour. He won three tournaments in the space of six weeks in 1984, including the prestigious World Series of Golf, and he tied for second in the 1985 US Open.*

CHAPTER FOUR
THE FINAL LEG OF THE GRAND SLAM

CHAPTER FOUR

THE FINAL LEG OF THE GRAND SLAM–

the US PGA Championship

The chip that Lee Trevino holed at Muirfield's 17th hole in 1972 to deny Tony Jacklin another British Open also robbed American observers of the prospect of Jack Nicklaus completing the Grand Slam, for the US PGA Championship has become the traditional fourth leg of the modern-day Grand Slam and when the 1972 version unfolded at Oakland Hills Country Club in Birmingham, a suburb of Detroit, the eyes of the world would otherwise have been firmly fixed on Nicklaus. That year the 'Golden Bear' had won the US Masters then the US Open and he was a strong favourite to take the third leg, the British Open, at Muirfield where he had won in 1966.

In fact it should have been Jacklin's championship because he was only 15 feet away in three at the long 17th on the last day and Trevino was standing on an embankment to the side of the green waiting to play his fifth shot. So when Trevino audaciously holed his chip it affected Jacklin to such an extent that he three-putted then moved on to the last hole and dropped another shot. Thus Nicklaus, back in the clubhouse following an astonishing 66, finished second – only one stroke behind Trevino.

What is more it cost the US PGA Championship a clear opportunity for its reputation as the poor relation of the other Grand Slam tournaments to be discarded at a time when feverish attempts were

being made to upgrade its status through the consistent use of respected courses such as Oakland Hills as the venue. This is because in its formative years the US PGA Championship was hawked to the highest bidder so that at times the event was staged at courses which simply could not be compared with Augusta or St Andrews.

In fact the Championship started life long before the Masters was invented. It was in January 1916 that Rodman Wanamaker, the son of a Philadelphia department store owner, met over lunch with several professionals and suggested that it was time they formed a PGA similar to that in Britain. Even so, it came into life a full 56 years after the British Open was born and 21 years after the first US Open had unfolded.

The decision to make the PGA Championship a match-play event

undoubtedly gave it a high place in the golfing calendar of the time. But the trouble was that it was open only to PGA members, which meant that the leading amateurs of the day, such as Bobby Jones, were automatically excluded.

So the US PGA Championship, like the US Masters, was not included in a modern-day Grand Slam for some time, since the considered opinion in the early years of the century was that the British Open and British Amateur coupled with the US Open and US Amateur should comprise the Grand Slam. That was achieved only once when the incomparable Jones, a modest man who never pondered on what he was going to do but simply went out and did it, took all four titles in 1930.

The astounding deeds of Jones meant that the US PGA Championship could only become

Previous spread Walking on water! Lee Trevino (left) and Gary Player at the 1984 US PGA Championship at Shoal Creek.

Right Oakland Hills, near Detroit, Michigan – venue of the US PGA Championship in 1972 and again in 1979.

Left The clubhouse at the Oakland Hills Country Club in Birmingham, a suburb of Detroit.

Below Lee Trevino, seen here chipping in at the 17th *en route* to victory in the 1972 British Open at Muirfield, grabbed glory again when he won the 1984 US PGA Championship.

established in a kind of vacuum from the moment when Jim Barnes, who came from Cornwall, beat Jock Hutchison, a Scotsman from St Andrews, by one hole in the first final in 1916. Moreover, since the American professionals at that time consisted mostly of British immigrants, there was a school of thought that they were merely hired help and it was amateurs like Jones who stole the attention of a sporting public eagerly attracted to the game.

By coincidence, the man who came to dominate the US PGA Championship in the 1920s was also the man who transformed the life of the professional golfer, since Walter Hagen was not prepared to walk in anybody's shadow.

Hagen won the US PGA in 1921. He then won the title four times in a row from 1924 and he also grasped four British Opens and two US Opens. 'The Haig,' as he became known, was not a classic

swinger but he possessed a formidable game on and around the green so that he was able time and time again to outgun opponents who might be overpowering him from tee to green. But it was Hagen's attitude that warmed the professional world because he would arrive from a late-night party in a chauffeur-driven limousine so that he could change into his elegant golfing gear in his own stylish manner at a time when professionals were not allowed in the clubhouse.

Hagen's approach to life was to 'smell the flowers along the way'. His high-living activities became almost as well documented as his golfing skills. He also needed to satisfy his expensive tastes, so Hagen demanded – and received – what were considered gargantuan sums at the time for exhibition matches and the like. In many respects these payments were the forerunner of appearance money – Seve Ballesteros, for instance, can demand around £50,000 to tee up in a sponsored event nowadays – and Gene Sarazen has voiced the opinion that every golf professional has Hagen to thank every time he

Above In the 1920s Walter Hagen won the US PGA five times and the British Open four times. Here, his wife embraces him at Hoylake in 1924 on the occasion of his second British Open win.

Right Seve Ballesteros, winner of the US PGA in 1980 and 1983, smiles despite the rain.

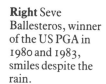

pops a cheque into his back pocket.

The Hagen era certainly provided the US PGA Championship with a degree of fame although it has lacked the presence of a strong international contingent in spite of South Africa's Gary Player winning the title both in 1962 and again ten years later when Nicklaus's Grand Slam dream had evaporated.

Tommy Armour was the last British-born player to succeed although by the time he scored his victory in 1930 he had moved over to representing America. Armour

had played for Britain in the Walker Cup of 1921 but as a professional he turned out for America in a match against Britain in 1925 that was considered a forerunner of the Ryder Cup.

He was born Thomas Dickson Armour in Edinburgh on 24 September 1896, and, having won the US Open in 1927, he followed his US PGA success – he edged out Gene Sarazen in the final – by winning the British Open at Carnoustie in 1931. During his playing days Armour became known as the 'Silver Scot' but he

RAYMOND FLOYD

'It was a phenomenal experience for me to be able to achieve one of my greatest desires since I was a little guy playing golf.' With those words, and with a few tears, Raymond Floyd greeted his victory in the 1986 US Open at Shinnecock Hills. He had played in the Championship on 21 previous occasions without ever being a contender. It seemed that was to be the case again in 1986 but Floyd notched three birdies in the last eight holes to move past a galaxy of rivals and win the championship, in racing parlance 'going away'. It was his 20th victory on the US PGA Tour – his first came in the St Petersburg Open in 1963 – and at the age of 43 years and nine months it made him the oldest US Open champion in the history of the championship. In fact, the previous oldest winner was the Englishman Ted Ray who won in 1920 at the age of 43 years, four months and 16 days. Moreover, it left him with only the British Open to win in order to complete a full collection of major championships.

Floyd had gained a reputation in the 1960s as a champagne-swilling, high-rolling golfer but this was outrageously over-exaggerated and he provided crystal-clear evidence of his golfing prowess by running away with the 1976 US Masters. He had already won the US PGA Championship in 1969 and he captured that title again in 1982 with an impressive performance. He began at Southern Hills, Tulsa, with a first round of 63 – seven under par – and he led all the way. He said: 'Without a doubt that 63 was the best round of golf I've ever played anywhere in my life.' His second and third round totals of 132 and 200 established US PGA Championship records and he missed the 72-holes record by just one shot after a double bogey at the last. Floyd, born in Fort Bragg, North Carolina, on 4 September 1942, is the son of an Army man who now co-owns the Cypress Lakes Golf Club in Fayetteville. He turned professional in 1961 and his victory in the 1986 US Open took his career earnings on the American circuit to 3,182,252 dollars.

Left 1982 was a particularly successful year for Ray Floyd during which he won the US PGA for the second time, on this occasion with a score of 262 at Southern Hills. Lanny Wadkins was runner-up.

he would not push himself through another seven days of match play. He might have been convinced by the PGA magazine report of 1948 which claimed: 'Hogan's methodical, businesslike manner of beating opponents did little to capture the gallery's fancy.'

In truth, it was felt by many observers that Hogan carried a huge chip on his shoulder. But it was his tenacity to succeed that drove him on, and into firm decisions such as refusing to play a round of golf with the King of Belgium because he was on holiday with his wife, Valerie, and that came first.

To explain Hogan's nine 'major championship' triumphs – six of which came after that near-fatal crash – one has to respect his single-mindedness. He was the son

Above Gary Player is one of the few non-American golfers to win the PGA; his victories came in 1962 and 1972. He is seen here at Shoal Creek in 1984 with his caddie 'Rabbit'.

gained a wider reputation for his coaching skills and even the great Bobby Jones once visited him to seek advice.

In the years following Hagen's domination of the Championship in the 1920s, the tournament was moved around several venues and was won by players with splendid names like Paul Runyan, Johnny Revolta, Denny Shute and Henry Picard.

Then, after the Second World War, it was the turn of Ben Hogan to start winning as he took the title in 1946 and 1948. Hogan missed

out in 1953, which was a pity for the Championship and the record books, since in that year he won the US Masters, the US Open and the British Open. In its way that was regarded as a Grand Slam performance so the US PGA Championship seemed condemned to being contested in the shadow of the other great events. Not that Hogan ignored it altogether for those two wins, in 1946 and then again two years later, provided ample evidence of his match-play skills but the great champion elected after his 1948 success to bypass the event.

Even though Hogan was involved in a near-fatal head-on collision with a bus in the spring of 1949, he had already decided at the end of the 1948 Championship that

'I had the composure. When you're choking and you've got a lot of pressure on you, your mouth gets very dry and you start spitting cotton . . . and I wasn't spitting cotton today.'

Lee Trevino on pressure (nearing his win in the 1984 US PGA Championship)

LANNY WADKINS

Lanny Wadkins is one of golf's most aggressive players. 'I get a kick out of playing that way,' he insists. 'I never take a bad risk but it's great to go for a par five with the second shot, especially over water. But every shot is calculated – I'm not just a thrasher.' You certainly don't win a US PGA Championship by 'thrashing' and that victory is what Wadkins achieved in 1977. He took the title in a play-off against the experienced Gene Littler at Pebble Beach and later that season he won the World Series of Golf. It enabled Wadkins to climb to third place in the official money list and that was to be his highest finish until 1985 when, with three impressive triumphs, he took second spot with a total of 15 victories on the American

tour. He belongs to the exclusive club of players who have competed in both the Walker and Ryder Cups.

Wadkins is considered by his rivals to be one of the toughest opponents around, but he was extremely disappointed at the 1985 Ryder Cup when he led off in the singles only to be beaten by Manuel Pinero. In fact, there have been a number of disappointments in his career. The prospect of another major championship coming his way has seemed likely on numerous occasions, but so often there was one player to beat him. For instance, he put in a tremendous eleventh-hour run in the 1986 US Open at Shinnecock Hills and then sat in the clubhouse for almost two hours to watch as Raymond Floyd alone came through to better his score. Even so, Wadkins has a marvellous

touch in windy conditions so he remains a likely contender for the British Open. He enjoyed a superb amateur career, for he won the US Amateur in 1970, and it was no surprise when he elected to turn professional in 1971. Born in Richmond, Virginia, on 5 December 1949, his special interests include fishing, swimming and hunting.

Left Lanny Wadkins won the PGA in 1977 after a play-off against Gene Littler. Here he has chipped in at the 11th at Shoal Creek, Alabama, during the 1984 tournament.

Above Wadkins made another valiant effort to capture a 'major' when he finished joint runner-up with Chip Beck behind Ray Floyd at the 1986 US Open.

HAL SUTTON

Born 28 April 1958, the son of an oilman, he won the US Amateur in 1980 and looked set to remain among the non-paid ranks when he joined his father's business. But he says: 'I started going as long as a month without playing. I had put so much into the game that I felt it senseless to give it all up. I can always go back into business. So I decided to turn pro.' In 1983 he proved that to be a sound decision when he won the Tournament Players Championship then the US PGA Championship.

He had already enjoyed a marvellous 'rookie' year by winning the Walt Disney World Golf Classic in 1982. He had eight top-ten

finishes that season and he banked 237,434 dollars. It was a sensational start and, although he had a lean year in 1984, he bounced right back in 1985 with two victories. He did not repeat his achievement of 1983, when he led the official money list, but it was a sign that all was well again with his game – he had nose-dived to 26th in 1984 – and in 1986 he quickly showed that he meant to continue his winning form. He won the Phoenix Open then captured the Memorial Tournament on Jack Nicklaus's tough Muirfield Village course – the scene of the 1987 Ryder Cup (see page 144). Although Sutton's father did not play golf, there is no doubt that he has been the moving force in his son's life. But it was a friend of

his father who sent Hal a set of clubs at the age of 11 and so started him on the way to fame and fortune of his own. 'I played some team sports but it was discouraging because I never seemed to be on a good team. I decided I wanted to win or lose on my own ability and that's why I chose golf.'

Below Hal Sutton launched himself on the road to super- stardom by winning the 1983 US PGA Championship.

of a blacksmith and, as a teenager, he would deal for the poker players so as to earn money by night to play golf by day.

Hogan, more than any other player, removed the human element from the game by refusing to stop practising even when his hands began to bleed. Such was his determination that his remedy for that particular inconvenience was to submerge his hands in brine then return to the practice range.

He stood up to pain well because in that car crash he suffered multiple injuries including a double fracture of the pelvis, broken ankle and ribs and the doctors were compelled to tie off the veins in his legs so as to counter the threat of blood clots. That Hogan ever played again was a miracle. That he enjoyed so much success was astonishing. But he remained absent from the PGA Championship and, as if because of his absence, the event began to lose its attraction to such an extent that the best venues refused to receive it and, elbowed along by television's demands, the inevitable switch to stroke play occurred in 1958 when Dow Finsterwald won.

It was two years later that the US PGA Championship received its biggest boost when Arnold Palmer invented the modern-day Grand Slam after following his 1960 US Masters win by taking the US Open at Cherry Hills in Denver.

Before Palmer set out for the British Open, with the prospect of emulating Hogan's achievement in 1953, he decided that there was a requirement for an even bigger challenge so he told observers of the game that the Grand Slam he was chasing added up to four titles

with the US PGA Championship included.

It was not to be, since Palmer was edged out of the British Open by Australia's Kel Nagle. But, whilst the PGA Championship was to remain elusive to Palmer, the tournament now had a place in the record books as the final leg of the Grand Slam.

Moreover it gained increasing popularity with Gary Player and Jack Nicklaus winning in 1962 and 1963 respectively and since Ray Floyd, Lee Trevino, Lanny Wadkins, Hal Sutton and Hubert Green are among the subsequent winners it clearly has a worthy roll-call of champions. What is more, Nicklaus won the title another four times in the ten years from 1970 so that it became another Championship that Jack built.

Today it remains the poor relation when compared with the other three major championships, but few who watched Trevino holding off Player in the 1984 version at Shoal Creek, or Trevino's attempt to overhaul Green and retain the title at Cherry Hills twelve months later, would not accept that the Championship had grown sufficiently in stature for its 70th anniversary in 1986 to have been celebrated in fine style.

Right Lee Trevino won the 1974 version at Tanglewood, North Carolina, then at Shoal Creek in 1984.

FALDO ON SAND SHOTS

The best tip for any beginner or a handicap golfer struggling with this part of his game is to go and see the local club professional. I am convinced that in one hour he will eliminate any fear you might have regarding bunker shots. And it is fear, first and foremost, which breeds sloppy shots in the sand.

My guide to good bunker play is to make sure you step into the sand both briskly and confidently. You have to feel that you are going to get that ball on to the green and close to the pin. It's honestly worth rehearsing such positive thoughts.

Now you are ready to play the

Left Keep your eyes and head down . . . and follow through!

shot. Take a really open stance and shuffle your feet into a solid and comfortable position. Next lay the angled face of the club so that it shines upwards and faces the hole and take a last look at the shot you intend to make. Remember not to ground the club because a bunker is a hazard and it is against the rules to touch the sand with the club before starting the backswing.

The swing? First you must realize that you cannot simply nip the ball off the top of the sand. Nor can you expect to splash the ball out towards the flag if you thrash the club at the sand as if you were killing snakes. You might move a bucketful of sand . . . but that's about all. What you must keep in mind is a full, slow, smooth backswing. Pick the club up

slightly with the right hand then accelerate downwards so that the sand wedge enters the sand between two to three inches behind the ball. The action will create a glancing blow from out to in which will bring the ball up quickly to land softly on the green. You must remember, too, to follow through for at least three feet and, of course, to keep your eyes and head down throughout the shot.

I confess that it is not the easiest shot in the world to play. But I must be honest and insist that too many amateurs build up a mental block against the shot. Go along to your local professional and I am sure that with his help, and with perseverance on your part, you will soon be exploding that ball out of the sand with better results.

The swing for a sand shot

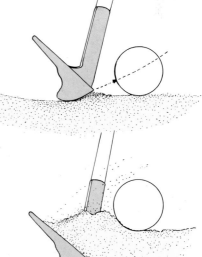

Incorrect – if the sole of the wedge merely slides across the surface of the sand, the ball will be topped and not lofted

Correct – the wedge enters the sand behind the ball and the gathered sand pushes the ball up sharply

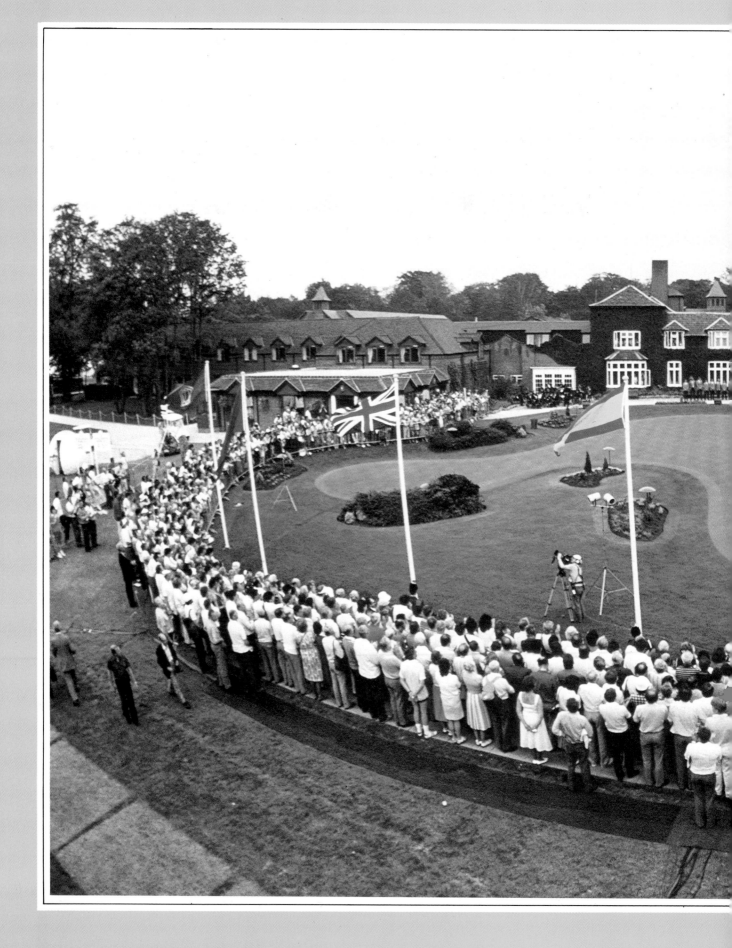

CHAPTER FIVE

THE NEW WORLD VERSUS THE OLD

CHAPTER FIVE

THE NEW WORLD VERSUS THE OLD -

the Ryder Cup and the Walker Cup

It was a scene which mirrored all that Sam Ryder ever wanted from the moment he presented an elegant golden chalice for regular competition between teams from Great Britain and Ireland and the United States of America. There was Jack Nicklaus with one emotive sweep of his arm plucking Tony Jacklin's ball marker from its spot some three feet from the hole on the last green at Royal Birkdale. And with that generous act Nicklaus not only conceded a putt ... he also conceded the prospect of America once again winning the Ryder Cup.

The year was 1969. Great Britain and Ireland had not won the biennial match since 1957. And Nicklaus, more than anybody watching that momentous afternoon, appreciated the pressure on Jacklin's shoulders. The same Tony Jacklin might have won the Open Championship two months earlier. And the same Tony Jacklin might have beaten – no, change that to thrashed – the mighty Nicklaus 4 and 3 that very morning in the first series of singles matches. But Nicklaus was well aware that this was the Ryder Cup, not a pot of gold for trousering in the back pocket, and that it was prestige which called the tune. He knew that if Jacklin had stood over that putt then in his mind it would have lengthened like the shadows as the sun started to set.

So Nicklaus gave Jacklin that putt. And the match finished tied at 16-16. If Nicklaus had not before

won the hearts of British supporters then he certainly went a long way to doing so that afternoon. The question for Nicklaus, as the 1987 golfing year approached, was whether or not he, or one of his compatriots, could afford to be anything like so generous as the latest edition of the Ryder Cup unfolded.

For Nicklaus the possibility of defeat, on his own Muirfield Village course at Dublin, Ohio, was

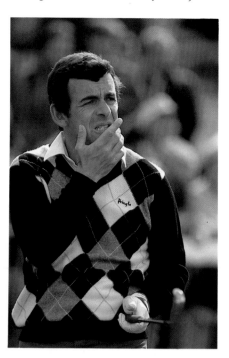

Above In the 1969 Ryder Cup, Tony Jacklin was relieved of the burden of holing a teasing putt when Jack Nicklaus conceded it, so that the match was tied 16-16.

Previous spread An aerial view of the

opening ceremony at the 1985 Bell's Scotch Ryder Cup.

Right Tony Jacklin sprays the fizz as (from left) Paul Way, Sam Torrance and Ian Woosnam applaud their supporters at The Belfry in 1985.

very much in his mind. He had not been at The Belfry in 1985 when Europe, amid scenes of historic, but understandable, bedlam, had overcome the power-hungry Americans by a whopping 16½-11½ margin.

Nicklaus had been responsible for elevating interest in the match in 1969. It required a stimulating gesture such as this. Every two years, the British and Irish boys had battered their heads against a brick wall as, try as they might, they met one defeat after another.

Moreover, Nicklaus's keenness to extend the Cup's life was evident from his suggested changes to foster greater competition and the introduction of the Continentals in 1979, so that the Americans now played a European team, certainly had his wholehearted support.

In 1983, when Nicklaus first wore the captain's hat, the progress of Spain's Severiano Ballesteros and then West Germany's Bernhard Langer provided the European team with a stronger backbone and the Americans squeezed through by the narrowest of margins. The decision of the British PGA, with the full backing of the US PGA, to introduce the Continentals had been justified. The match was alive and well.

Some observers insist that Nicklaus anticipated defeat at The Belfry and that he elected to stand down as captain. In truth it cannot be looked upon in that way because in recent times the American system has been to pass on the

ROYAL LYTHAM AND ST ANNES

A premier seaside course where any lack of natural attractiveness is more than made up by constant challenges to ability and judgement. Success derives from straight driving and keeping the ball on the fairways.

Above Tony Jacklin making his speech after winning the 1969 British Open at Royal Lytham and St Annes. Jack Nicklaus is pictured third from left

CARD OF THE COURSE

OUT			IN		
HOLE	YARDS	PAR	HOLE	YARDS	PAR
1	206	3	10	334	4
2	420	4	11	485	5
3	458	4	12	189	3
4	393	4	13	339	4
5	188	3	14	445	4
6	486	5	15	468	4
7	551	5	16	356	4
8	394	4	17	413	4
9	162	3	18	386	4
	3258	35		3415	36
			TOTAL	6673	71

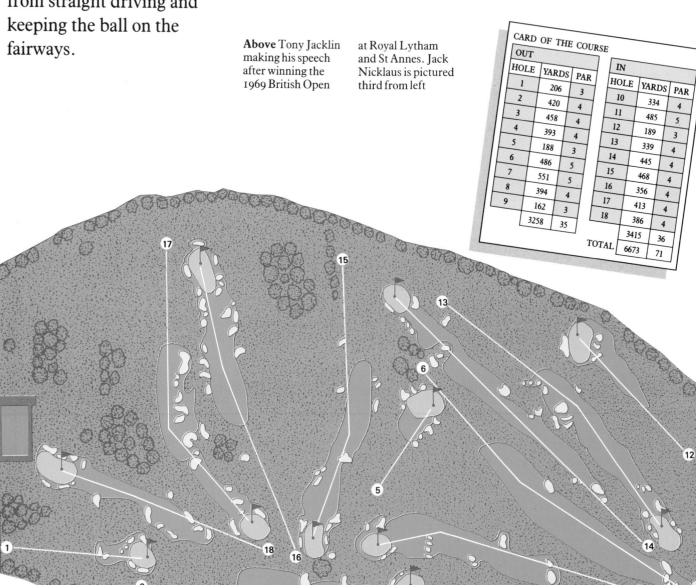

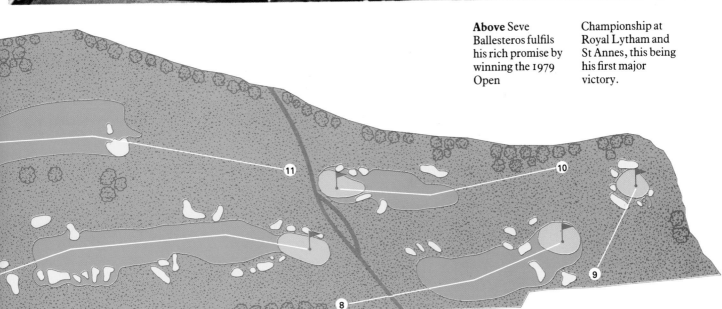

Above Seve Ballesteros fulfils his rich promise by winning the 1979 Open Championship at Royal Lytham and St Annes, this being his first major victory.

HOWARD CLARK

With a marvellous season in 1986 Howard confirmed his arrival as one of the finest British golfers in the modern-day era. Yet the Yorkshireman, following two wins in three weeks in 1978, went into a decline from which it seemed he might not escape. Clark, the British Boys' Champion in 1971, turned professional in 1973, shortly after winning Walker Cup honours, then made gradual progress. He captured the Portuguese Open then the Madrid Open in the spring of 1978 and, having made his Ryder Cup debut the previous year, it seemed that he was destined to rise to the top. But the maturing process took longer than most anticipated and Clark, despite playing again in the Ryder Cup in 1981, did not triumph again until 1984. Once more, things slipped nicely into place in the Madrid Open and, after that win, Clark was a changed man. He began to adopt a more philosophical outlook on his golf, no longer turning a drama into a crisis, and he emphasized his reformed ways by winning the 1984 Whyte and Mackay PGA Championship at Wentworth. Thus Clark climbed to third spot in the Order of Merit and, although falling back to sixth in 1985, he maintained his winning form with victories in the Jersey and Glasgow Opens. His success in Glasgow came when he chipped in to beat Sandy Lyle, who had won the Open Championship one month earlier, in a sudden-death play-off. Then he gained world-wide acclaim by being the individual winner in the World Cup at La Quinta, California, two months after helping Europe win the Ryder Cup against the United States. It was clear that Clark meant to continue his winning ways as he breezed into 1986 with victories in the Madrid Open and the Peugeot Open.

Left Howard Clark keeps a careful eye on the ball during the 1985 Whyte and Mackay PGA Championship at Wentworth. His 1984 victory was not to be repeated, though.

honour of being captain to a new man every match. That Nicklaus is back in 1987 is significant.

He will, of course, be the captain on his own course. More importantly, he has been 'selling' the match to an American public who in the past have treated it with such contempt that in newspaper terms it barely rates a paragraph. In Britain, of course, the 1985 victory was one of the major sporting stories of the year.

Nicklaus is gathering the support he knows that his team members will need, and which they missed at The Belfry where almost 80,000 walked the fairways in three days, to keep morale high in the knowledge that the European players have no intention of relinquishing the Cup.

He is well aware, too, that he will need to inject passion and fire into the bellies of the American golfers. That is where, on this occasion, he will need to match Jacklin. For whereas Jacklin, back for a third successive time as captain, galvanized his players at The Belfry, Lee Trevino failed to generate in his team the same camaraderie which existed among the Europeans and which carried them on to an emotional triumph.

In fact Europe made an inauspicious start. Manuel Pinero and Seve Ballesteros, launching a partnership that would play a vital part in the victory, beat Curtis Strange and Mark O'Meara in the opening foursomes match. But the Americans won each of the other three foursomes, so that at lunch the Europeans were 3-1 down.

Jacklin, as brave a captain as he was a player, risked possible criticism at the end of the day. He dropped Sandy Lyle, the new British Open champion, and he put the out-of-form Paul Way together with Ian Woosman for the first of the four fourballs in the afternoon. For Jacklin the gamble paid off so handsomely that he must have felt as if he had picked a 20-1 Derby winner.

Way and Woosnam, playing some inspired golf, sank the experienced partnership of Fuzzy Zoeller and Hubert Green. It was a personal triumph for Way, troubled for months with tonsillitis, who calmly holed a putt of eleven feet on the last green to secure a vital point, proving wrong those

Below Tony Jacklin, Europe's 1985 Ryder Cup captain, cheers on 'tiny tots' Paul Way and Ian Woosnam.

Right Craig Stadler's missed putt during the morning of the second day boosted European confidence as the 1985 Ryder Cup unfolded at The Belfry.

as foolhardy and futile – that the spectators went overboard in support of the home team. Some American observers were even embarrassed by these timid excuses. It is no different in any land, as the Americans should know full well, especially now after the way the Masters crowd cheered Nicklaus past Ballesteros with such justifiable enthusiasm at Augusta in 1986.

The Americans, however, were reeling at The Belfry. That was immediately evident when the next series of foursomes began on the afternoon of the second day. The Spaniards José-María Cañizares and José Rivero, who had been selected by Jacklin in the face of some criticism, pounded Tom Kite and Calvin Peete to a 7 and 5 defeat. Ballesteros and Pinero regained

who felt he should have withdrawn.

Ballesteros and Pinero won again and that evening, when Bernhard Langer and José-María Cañizares had squeezed a half out of the formidable Craig Stadler and Hal Sutton, so Europe could rest easier in the knowledge that they had reduced the American lead to 4½-3½.

In the fourballs series the following morning Way and Woosnam continued where they left off, again defeating Zoeller and Green, and Howard Clark and Sam Torrance formed a winning partnership. Ballesteros and Pinero, however, lost their unbeaten record and the attention swung on to the last match to finish before lunch. Jack had brought together Langer, the US Masters champion, and Lyle, the British Open Champion. But when Curtis Strange, partnered by Stadler, drilled a six-iron shot to within a foot of the hole at the 16th the

European cause seemed lost. Langer and Lyle played the 17th two down, knowing that they could not win and that half a point in such circumstances would be a miracle, but somehow the gods were kind. Lyle, retaining his nerve under the ensuing pressure, confidently found the sanctuary of the cup with a putt of fully 20 feet at the 17th to halve the deficit. Stadler, with a putt of little more than 18 inches to secure victory on the last green, contrived to miss and turned away in horror.

Stadler's indecision at such a crucial time inspired the Europeans and raised a doubt in the minds of the Americans. The overall score now stood at 6-6 and the Americans were not only being teased and tormented on the fairways, they were also finding the partisan support of the crowd too much. There were to be complaints from some of the Americans later – complaints that should be regarded

winning form by thrashing the crestfallen Stadler and Sutton 5 and 4. Then Ken Brown linked with Langer to beat Ray Floyd and Lanny Wadkins 3 and 2. Way and Woosnam suffered their only defeat together but Europe closed the day with a 9-7 advantage.

The total number of points at stake in the match was 28, so when Jacklin woke the following morning, virtually numbed by the brilliant performance of his players, he knew that the Europeans required only 5½ points from the 12 singles remaining to secure a famous win. It sounded easy, although it most certainly should not have been on all previous form. Yet from the moment that Pinero took on the effervescent Wadkins and pushed him towards a 3 and 1 defeat, so the afternoon became a

Left In 1979 continental players, including Severiano Ballesteros, took part in the Ryder Cup for the first time as Europe united against the Americans.

Below (inset) Bernhard Langer is another valuable continental addition to the Ryder Cup team. He is seen here during the 1983 version at the PGA National Golf Club, Palm Beach Gardens, Florida. (Main picture) Water, water, everywhere – and much else besides. Langer seems, however, to have overcome an awkward lie at the 6th in 1983.

victory march for the Europeans and a wake for the Americans.

Stadler recovered some self-respect by beating Woosnam. Langer, however, quickly shut the door on Sutton 5 and 4, and Lyle moved past Peter Jacobsen 3 and 2. Way, keeping his cool, refused to be shaken by the experienced Floyd and when the American found a watery grave at the 18th it meant that Europe were within 1½ points of success. Ballesteros claimed the half point with as gutsy a finish as one would expect from the extraordinary Spaniard. With

three birdies in five holes from the 13th, he clawed his way back to all-square against Tom Kite, who had been leading three up.

To European golf enthusiasts every member of the team on that astonishing afternoon would be hailed as a hero but the glory of gaining the decisive point had to fall to one of them. In the end, though Clark and Cañizares also won, it came down to Torrance. The Scot had been three down with eight holes to play. Yet he launched a dramatic recovery, holing from six feet to square the match at the

Above Sam Torrance got up and down from 60 yards at the last hole in the 1983 Ryder Cup, forcing Tom Kite to accept a half.

Right The sky's the limit – and that's the way it proved for Tony Jacklin and his European Ryder Cup team in 1985.

'We've proved the gap is closing. In 1983 we almost got there – I was happy and numb. The guys had courage – there wasn't a gripe, not a problem. We knew then that in 1985 the Americans would fear us. And they did.'

Tony Jacklin on his Ryder Cup team

Above The magnificent Ryder Cup.

Right Tony Jacklin (centre) congratulates Bernhard Langer and Nick Faldo after they had collected their third point from four matches in the 1983 Ryder Cup.

17th then completing the business with a flourish by rolling in a putt of 22 feet for a winning birdie on the 18th green. The galleries erupted, the champagne flowed and Torrance stood on the last green, arms raised in triumph, as the fans acknowledged a supreme achievement.

Sam had won it for Sam (Ryder that is, rather than Uncle Sam!). The Ryder Cup would stay, at least for two years, on the 'right' side of the Atlantic. It was the biggest defeat inflicted upon the Americans since the series started in 1927. It was the first 'home' win since Lindrick in 1957. Samuel Ryder, who started the match, had died in 1936 at the age of 77, but Mrs Joan Ryder Scarfe, his youngest daughter, was present at The Belfry in 1986. Sadly, she died only

a few weeks after the victory.

In truth, it can be said that the match had its beginnings some six years before the United States won the inaugural contest by a 9½-2½ margin at Worcester, Massachusetts. The Americans had insisted on bringing a team over for a match at Gleneagles, in Scotland, so as to test the strength of their players against the British. Most Scots shared the same opinion – 'they dinna regaird it as a lee-vel match'. They were right – and the Americans were soundly thrashed 9-3.

There was to be a second informal match, at Wentworth in 1926, when the Americans suffered greater humiliation by losing 13½-1½, but the difference on that occasion was the presence of a certain Samuel Ryder. Now young

Samuel had started his working life in the family's corn-chandler business in Manchester. There he had the idea that they should sell seeds in penny packets rather than by weight. It was a suggestion that fell upon deaf ears. So Samuel packed his bags and headed south to St Albans where he was to start a business that was to prosper as his penny packets became all the rage.

Samuel had one other love – golf. He put together that second informal match then agreed to a suggestion by George Duncan, the 1920 British Open champion, that he should offer a trophy for regular competition between the two golfing nations on either side of the Atlantic. He underwrote the travel expenses of the GB and Ireland team for the first official match but, more importantly, he commissioned the designing and casting of the beautiful golden chalice which bears his name.

There was little doubt that the Americans were learning fast as they won that first official match in 1927. Great Britain and Ireland, however, managed to win in 1929 and 1933, so that Samuel Ryder did experience success. In fairness to the man he never meant the match to act as a kind of barometer for measuring the difference between the standard of the game in Britain and Ireland compared with that in America. To Ryder it was simply a friendly encounter and he would probably have seen little point himself in changing the basis of competition by introducing the Continentals.

Below The victorious American team with the Ryder Cup in 1983.

The format, too, of the Ryder Cup has changed over the years but since 1979 it has remained the same. On the first day there are four fourballs in the afternoon, and on the following day this procedure is reversed. Then there follows the twelve singles. There is a chance that the format might be manipulated for television purposes at Muirfield Village as the Americans become more and more aware of the match through Nicklaus's efforts. The captain's role, once the match starts, is to link together in foursomes two compatible players since, especially as they alternate in striking the ball, it is quite likely that if one gets into trouble the other will have come across the situation himself! In fourballs it is not quite so important to have this sort of pairing as both of them play their

own ball throughout the game.

The captain must also keep his team sharp and well disciplined, honing them for what has become an increasingly strenuous contest, whilst at the same time ensuring that the true spirit of what Samuel Ryder set out to achieve is maintained.

Yet whilst Nicklaus's gesture in 1969 in conceding that putt to Jacklin captivated the audience, it is doubtful whether Sam Snead, the American captain, was so appreciative of Nicklaus's generous gesture. For the late Eric Brown, the GB and Ireland captain, had left no doubt on the eve of the match about his instructions to his players. Brown bellowed: 'Our players will not have the time to look for American golf balls lost in the rough.'

That was Brown. A true fighter.

TOM KITE

His victory in the 1985 Tournament of Champions was nothing less than the Texan – he was born in McKinney on 9 December 1949 – deserved. Kite, who turned professional in 1972 after making the Walker Cup team and sharing the NCAA title with his University of Texas team-mate Ben Crenshaw, is a better player than his record would suggest. His success in the Tournament of Champions was only the eighth of his career but in 1981 he was the leading money winner in America with 375,699 dollars and a stroke average of 69.80. Tom, encouraged by his father, first hit a shot at the age of six.

When he was 11 he won his first tournament, an age-group event at the Country Club in his home town of Austin, Texas. It was to be three years, however, before he was to take the game seriously and embark on a route that would lead to him becoming one of the finest professionals on the American circuit. In 1970 he showed rich potential by finishing runner-up to Lanny Wadkins in the US Amateur and second in the Southern Amateur, then winning the Western Amateur before being selected to the US team for the World Amateur Team Championship.

There are few more consistent golfers from America than Kite although he has often snatched defeat from the jaws of victory in the major championships. He had his chance in the British Open in 1985 but he faltered after reaching the turn in the lead on the last day. Then, at Augusta in 1986, he had the chance to hole a putt on the last green but missed, so failing to take Jack Nicklaus into a play-off. Here, as so often for him, fate seemed to be against him as he struck what looked like the perfect putt only to see the ball edge away from the hole at the last moment, once again denying Kite a place in the history books.

Left Tom Kite was one of the American Ryder Cup team in 1983 who felt increasingly hard-pressed by their British opponents.

MUIRFIELD VILLAGE

Swinging round the venue for the 1987 Ryder Cup

This is where Europe will defend the Bell's Scotch Ryder Cup in 1987, and a very demanding course it is too. Not that one would expect anything else, as this is 'Jack's course' . . . built by the maestro and the home of Nicklaus's own tournament, called The Memorial. It's tough not only because it is a

severe golf course but also because of the capricious breezes that they get in Dublin, Ohio. In fact, it can blow very hard, so club selection is of paramount importance. When Hal Sutton won The Memorial in 1986 with a record score of 271, conditions were fabulous.

I believe it is the toughest 'second-shot' golf course that I've ever played. The severity of the contours on the greens, coupled with the places they put the pins, make it

can start looking for birdies, as the greens are so pure. But if you make any mistakes there are simply no bale-out areas on the course. If you start missing greens then you'd better hope that your short game is in great shape. Sometimes it is better to be in

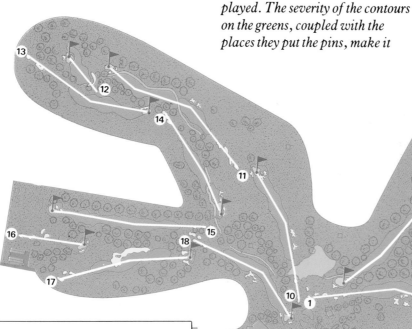

Right Looking towards the third hole at Muirfield Village, scene of the 1987 Ryder Cup.

CARD OF THE COURSE		
OUT		
HOLE	YARDS	PAR
1	446	4
2	452	4
3	392	4
4	204	3
5	531	5
6	430	4
7	549	5
8	189	3
9	410	4
	3603	36

IN		
HOLE	YARDS	PAR
10	441	4
11	538	5
12	158	3
13	442	4
14	363	4
15	490	5
16	204	3
17	430	4
18	437	4
	3503	36
TOTAL	7106	72

almost impossible to get it close unless you are in absolutely outstanding form. If you can position the ball on the correct side of the greens from which to putt then you

the bunkers, where you can impart some spin on the ball, rather than in the rough around the greens out of which it is virtually impossible to stop the ball accurately once it reaches the green.

Hole 1: *A left to right dog-leg which you play downhill. There is a creek which runs in among the trees down the left side and a couple of bunkers perched on the side of the hill. The fairway slopes from right to left, so you drive almost at the bunkers and let the ball kick in and run down. From there you need a medium- to long-iron into a green which is heavily guarded. This green is down at the bottom of an incline coming from right to left, running down towards the creek, with bunkers down the left. There is a plateau at the front, then the land falls downwards to form the rest of the green. If the pin is on the left side, then the putt is very, very fast.*

Hole 2: *The next hole is quite the opposite. The fairway slopes from left to right with a creek running down the right side all the way to the green where it widens out into a pool. You need a driver off the tee but, when the fairways are firm, you must hit it down the left-hand side of the fairway, fairly tight to the trees, in order to ensure that the ball doesn't kick down towards the trees. Quite a long second shot, with something like a 4-iron, into a very small, flattish green.*

Hole 3: *A lovely hole – a dog-leg, moving to the left. The idea is to hit the ball up the right side of the fairway, probably with a 3-wood, and stay clear of the left where you can be blocked out by some trees. The kidney-shaped green is in between a couple of oak trees, with the fat bit on the front left side going up to a very, very small back right section. If you play left into the fat part of the green, then you will*

simply leave yourself a tremendously difficult putt as there is a ridge, rather like a spine, moving across the green. It probably needs a 6- or a 7-iron to the back corner, or a 9-iron if the pin is at the front.

Hole 4: *The first short hole which requires about a 4-iron. There are bunkers all the way up the right side. The green slopes right to left, where there is a sheer drop into the trees. A typical Nicklaus hole, as a faded long-iron is the perfect shot.*

Hole 5: *A very interesting hole, requiring a left to right smash off the tee. The hole turns sharply from left to right, with the stream running up the middle of what is, therefore, a split fairway. You can make it in two with a good 3-wood. Or you can go up the right side of the fairway to the edge of the green or, on the left side of the stream, there is a chunk of fairway where you can play across with a medium-iron for safety and then wedge to the green. It depends where the pin has been put – but there are plenty of options to keep you thinking.*

Hole 6: *A very wide, generous fairway, and after a good drive you need about a 5-iron to the green which is in some ways guarded by a lake, although it should not come too much into play. There is a trap at the front of the green, which is more likely to catch the ball, but although it is a long hole two good shots here could lead to a birdie.*

Hole 7: *You tee off up in the corner of this par five, firing the ball between trees with the intention of carrying a trap on the left. By going up the left side you have an outside chance of reaching the green in two. But as the fairway also runs out before the green, most players take an iron for their second with the aim of giving themselves a suitable shot into a very fast green.*

Hole 8: *The next of the short holes and another tricky one. It's about a 7-iron to the front and possibly a 4 or 5 if the pin is on the back. You play the shot through an avenue of trees to a very slim green, with traps all the way down the front left. You can easily stray into the bunkers.*

Hole 9: *The fairway contours its way through an avenue of trees, forcing you to take a driver because the green is again extremely narrow. As you play to it over water then you want to be hitting as short an iron as possible. If you miss the green by just a foot on the left side and the pin is on the left, then you have no shot – it's that brutal a hole. So if you are hitting in with something like an 8- or 9-iron you at least have the chance of hitting an accurate shot simply to ensure a par.*

Hole 10: *A long hole, where you drive up a hill with bunkers on the left. Then, if you've hit the ball far enough, it's a long iron into a green guarded left and right by traps. The green is quite big and you don't want to be past the pin or you will have a very fast and nasty putt back.*

Hole 11: *This hole, in my opinion, is a little unfair. There is a creek which runs across the fairway and the long hitters probably cannot risk a driver. The creek starts by running down the left, then crosses the fairway before turning again to run down the right side, ending up in front of the green. The hole has a slight S-shape to it and the green is raised up above the creek so it is quite difficult to stop the pitch. There is also a very deep bunker front left.*

Hole 12: *An evil par three, with a big lake as the focal point. You are hitting downhill through an avenue of trees, with the wind swirling, so it is very important to be accurate. The hole, like the third, has a kidney-shaped green with an unbelievably thin back right section (only 20 feet wide). If you knock it into the back*

left bunker then you face a horrifying shot with the green running away from you towards the water. In fact, I've seen players chip the ball forward in the bunker so as to get themselves closer to the green to play out with a simple 'power-puff' shot. If you attempt to go at any bunker and chip shot from around the green then it's quite likely that the ball will run straight down into the water. It requires something between an 8- and a 6-iron for the tee shot.*

Hole 13: *A left-hand dog-leg where, once again, you drive through the trees and then play slightly downhill to the green. This slopes right to left with a bunker all the way down the right side. You must not hit anything right or you have virtually no shot, as the green falls away and then drops off to the left. It is quite a long hole and with a medium iron into the green it is another where you are happy to come out of with a par.*

Hole 14: *There is a creek which runs down the left side of this hole then across the fairway diagonally from left to right. So most players go with an iron or a small wood off the tee, leaving themselves a wedge or a 9-iron into a very small, finger-shaped green. There are severe bunkers up the left side of the green and if you go into them, although you are no more than 15 feet from the green, it requires a really excellent shot to keep the ball on the putting surface when splashing out. In fact, and I am not exaggerating, I think it is impossible to keep it on the green from out of that bunker.*

Hole 15: *A par five through the trees which is all uphill. You need to*

drive the ball a long way to be able to go for the green in two. If not, then you are faced with a very precarious lay-up into a kind of valley, or dip, with humps and hollows in the dark, shady area provided by the giant trees. And just beyond all this is the creek in front of the hill-top green. Even so, I rate this hole a birdie chance.*

Hole 16: *This is a straightforward hole where you simply hit two solid shots. It requires no more than that and it has less character than any of the others.*

Hole 17: *A boomerang-shaped trap running in front of you across the fairway and then up the left-hand side must be avoided, although the fairway is reasonably generous. But you shoot the second at a very severe green. There is a trap on the right which is like a pot bunker – a good six feet deep – and the green is guarded by other bunkers. The hole can quite often play downwind and the green can get incredibly hard. In these circumstances it becomes very hard to stop the ball even if you are going in with a wedge.*

Hole 18: *I am surprised that Jack built a finishing hole which requires a 3-wood rather than a driver off the tee. The creek runs down the left side here, then turns to the right again and starts going up the hill. There is no point trying to cut the corner off, with bunkers down the right, so after a good 3-wood you leave yourself about a 5-iron into a green guarded by some steep traps. The green is not too severe, but you don't want to hit the ball past the hole or you have a fast putt back.*

CALVIN PEETE

Born in Detroit, Michigan, on 18 July 1943, he spent most of his formative years on a Florida farm with his 18 brothers and sisters. Sold clothes, watches, rings – anything – to migrant farm workers to make a living. In 1966, at the age of 23, he tried his hand at golf for the first time. 'I read that Jack Nicklaus was making 200,000 dollars a year and I reckoned that I would be happy with one third that sum,' recalls Peete, 'so it was worth a try.' Broke through with 1979 Greater Milwaukee Open win and moved on his way to two million dollars in official earnings with victories in 1985 Phoenix Open and Tournament Players Championship.

There can be no question of Peete's ability to sustain his performance, as in 1986 he enjoyed another astonishing season which he launched by winning the Tournament of Champions then the USF&G Classic. That took his number of victories in seven years to twelve and he also passed the magical two-million-dollar mark in official winnings on the US PGA Tour. Yet it was in 1984 that he surpassed even his wildest dreams, for when he had two rounds of 66 and two of 67 en route to winning the Texas Open in San Antonio, it assured him of his first Vardon Trophy for the low stroke average of the year – 70.56 to be exact. He said: 'Winning the Vardon Trophy would be like winning a tournament so, today, I feel as if I have won twice.' He was also greatly honoured to make the United States Ryder Cup team in 1983 and he retained his place in the side in 1985.

Below Calvin Peete took his prize winnings to more than two million dollars during the 1986 campaign.

Above Arnold Palmer: 'When you stand on the tee at a Ryder Cup match . . . your stomach rumbles . . .'.

Palmer is pictured here taking part in the 1971 version at St Louis, Missouri, which the US team won by 18½-13½.

A speak-as-you-find-it man with ice-blue eyes and a viper-like tongue. This time his words were designed to galvanize his men – to convince them that the Americans, in spite of names like Nicklaus, Trevino and Casper, could be outgunned. Well, Brown went some way to achieving that – and so, as the years rolled on, and

Jacklin became the captain for the matches in 1983 and 1985, there was increasing evidence that the class chasm between America and Europe was being appreciably narrowed.

Yet, returning to 1969, relationships between the teams, despite Brown's typical approach, were normalized and the one outstanding memory of that nail-biting week on the Lancashire coast was quite simply that even if the Ryder Cup isn't worth a penny or a cent to the winners, its spirit remained alive and well even in an

era which was to open the proverbial floodgates to amazing increases in prize funds made available at tournaments.

As Arnold Palmer once claimed: 'It doesn't matter how many Open Championships or titles you may have won. When you stand on a tee at a Ryder Cup match, playing for your country, your stomach rumbles like that of a kid turning up for his first tournament.'

On the other hand it could be argued that Palmer went to great lengths in 1967 to make certain that one of the 'enemy' suffered a few collywobbles. The setting was Houston, Texas, and Palmer, whose biggest love next to golf and his family is flying, took the amiable and apparently fearless George Will for a spin in his private plane. What transpired was that Palmer rather overdid the skylarks so that poor George reappeared ashen-faced from the plane, looking like Marcel Marceau . . . and saying about as much!

Not that Palmer escaped scot-free. He had unfortunately chosen that particular Ryder Cup when America had the formidable Ben Hogan as their captain. And the fact that Hogan left the hero-worshipped Palmer, who had gathered two points on the first day, out of the morning fourballs on the second day provided sufficient evidence of his feeling on the subject.

Yet even a flyaholic like Palmer would have found his nerve put to a severe test if he had been aboard the plane which took the Great Britain and Ireland team on from Los Angeles to Palm Springs for the 1959 match at Eldorado Country Club. The flight on the twin-engined airliner was expected to take 40 minutes – instead it developed into a 90-minute nightmare as a violent electrical storm tossed the plane around like a cork above the jagged peaks of the San Jacinto Mountains.

The late Ron Heager, then the *Daily Express* golf correspondent, was on board with the players and he cabled: 'We were tossed around like a cocktail in a shaker . . . From our flying height of 13,000 feet we dropped like a stone to 9,000 feet. It was like falling in a giant lift when the cable had snapped. Only . . . your stomach stayed on the tenth storey. It was the Big Dipper – without the laughs.'

There was also little joy on the fairways that year for GB and Ireland, as they lost 8½-3½, but The Belfry signalled a gigantic swing in fortunes and the Europeans, with the Swedish golfers also making significant progress, will be hoping to win for

the first time on American soil when the match unfolds at Muirfield Village.

In the amateur game the equivalent of the Ryder Cup is the Walker Cup, which in 1987 will be played at Sunningdale, and as far as this match is concerned Great Britain and Ireland have had little success with only two wins and one draw out of 25 starts. The psychological barrier has grown so that the Americans now start each match in the kind of relaxed manner that if adopted by Great Britain and Ireland could well work in their favour.

Today's youngsters, of course, are in a hurry to turn professional and so they are already hardening themselves to that cause as they play Walker Cup golf before moving over to the paid ranks. Their objective, as individual players, is to prove that they can batter into submission an American opponent whom they one day

---

'I would have loved to have played in the Walker Cup. The trouble was that when the team for 1975 was chosen I was an unknown. Eight months later I had won 11 amateur titles. And by 1977, when the next Walker Cup was played, I was a professional.'

Nick Faldo on the Walker Cup

Right Five-times winner of both the British and the English Amateur Championships, Michael Bonallack made nine successive Walker Cup appearances from 1957 to 1973. Here in the 1971 version at St Andrews, he anxiously watches the progress of his putt.

EUROPE'S BEST

Gordon Brand *A true Yorkshireman, he captured the Nigerian Open and Ivory Coast Open, each for a second time, on the Safari circuit in 1986 – though he climbed a more prestigious Everest back in 1983, when he won a place in Europe's Ryder Cup team.*

Gordon Brand Jnr *Followed an excellent amateur career, during which time he played in the Walker Cup, by winning twice during his first year as a professional in 1982. More importantly, he won the Panasonic European Open at Sunningdale in 1984. He is a Scottish World Cup player.*

Andrew Chandler *A journeyman professional who gained a breakthrough by winning the São Paulo International Classic through equalling the course record with a last round 63 in Brazil, then played with renewed vigour on the 1986 PGA European Tour.*

Roger Chapman *Won the English Amateur Championship in 1979, then graduated to Walker Cup honours two years later. He has made steady progress as a professional and had only 24 putts in a round of 61, including an outward 29, in the 1985 Ebel European Masters at Crans-sur-Sierre, Switzerland.*

Neil Coles (MBE) *The first of more than 31 European tour wins for Coles came in the 1956 Gor-Ray Tournament. He has challenged for the Open Championship, too, on several occasions – finishing joint second behind Tom Weiskopf at Troon in 1973. He celebrated his 50th birthday in 1984, but what might he have achieved if an aversion to flying had not restricted his travelling?*

Eamonn Darcy *As a youngster he nursed the burning ambition to become a jockey but the genial Irishman turned to golf instead. He has enjoyed greater success overseas than in his native Ireland, winning the 1981 West Lakes Classic in Australia and the 1983 Spanish Open.*

David Feherty *The son of a travel agent from Bangor, Northern Ireland, Feherty scored his first professional success in the ICL International on the South African 'sunshine' circuit. But he enjoyed a more important breakthrough when he won the Italian Open at Albarella, near Venice, in 1986.*

Anders Forsbrand *Bjorn Borg and Mats Wilander have given Sweden a strong hold in the tennis arena, but Forsbrand is one of a promising group of players from that country who are fast making their names in the world of golf. He has represented his country in the World Cup and he enjoyed a fine week in the Epson Grand Prix in 1986 when he beat Sandy Lyle for third place.*

Bernhard Gallacher *Topped the Order of Merit in 1969 and opened the door to an illustrious career. A regular winner, and a Ryder Cup player from 1969 to 1983 inclusive, Gallacher has failed to channel his fighting capabilities into a significant Open challenge. He now combines the life of touring professional with a club job at Wentworth.*

Antonio Garrido *Returned to form in 1986 when he won the London Standard Four Stars National Pro-Celebrity event at Moor Park. That success took his prize winnings in European earnings to more than £250,000 since turning professional in 1961 at the age of 17. He has also won the Spanish Open (1972), Madrid Open (1977), Benson and Hedges International (1977) and Tunisian Open (1982).*

Left Gordon Brand Jnr – a top hope for Ryder Cup honours in 1987.

Mark James *From 1976 to 1981 he finished three times as Britain's leading player in the Open Championship. Like many golfers in the modern age he graduated from the Walker Cup (1975) to the Ryder Cup. Successive victories in the Carrolls Irish Open, at Portmarnock in 1979 and 1980, emphasized that he produces his best golf on linksland.*

Michael King *After turning to the professional game relatively late in life at the age of 25, he earned the respect of his colleagues by becoming a Ryder Cup player in 1979. He also won the Tournament Players Championship that year at Moor Park. He has considerable ability but has not proved himself a big occasion player – yet.*

Above Bernard Gallacher was unable to beat Tom Watson in the 1983 Ryder Cup.

Below Mark James watches his ball's progress during the 1984 Open at St Andrews.

Robert Lee *A young golfer with a very promising future. He won the Cannes Open in 1985 then the Brazilian Open later in the year. In 1985 he also equalled a world record by covering nine holes in 27 strokes on the way to a 61 in the Johnnie Walker Monte Carlo Open at Mont Agel. An England Youth International in 1982, he breezed into 1986 brimming with confidence and soon demonstrated his potential once again.*

David Llewellyn *A super-cool Welshman who loves life, he relaxes by reading Shakespeare. Between winning the Kenya Open in 1972 and the Ivory Coast Open in 1985 he led a nomadic existence, moving through several different jobs including one at a club in Malta. He was 'rookie of the year' in 1971 and a Welsh World Cup player in 1974 and again in 1985.*

Michael McLean *Many observers now believe that he has served his apprenticeship, since turning professional in 1981, and that he could emerge in the second half of the 1980s as one of Britain's finest golfers. His baby face camouflages an intense will to succeed.*

Carl Mason *He sprang from his usual role as a member of the supporting cast by charging into fourth place in the Open Championship at Muirfield in 1980. Too often he has suffered from lack of belief in himself, but he appears to have more confidence now. He won the Lusaka Open in 1975 and the Zambia Open in 1984.*

Christy O'Connor Jnr *A Ryder*

Cup player in 1975, this genial Irishman thought he should have made the team again in 1985. He certainly enjoyed a marvellous season in which he was tied third in the Open Championship and claimed four other top-ten places. However, he narrowly failed to earn his place through the Order of Merit and he was not one of the three players selected by Tony Jacklin.

José-María Olazábal *A young Spaniard with a rich amateur pedigree, Olazábal took the Spanish and Italian titles in 1983 and then, after collecting the British Boys' the same year, went on to win the Amateur Championship at Formby in 1984, and the British Youths' the following year. He turned professional and won the PGA European Tour qualifying school at La Manga, then soon made his mark on the circuit in 1986.*

John O'Leary *His success in the*

Above Robert Lee is fast making his name on the international scene.

Below Peter Oosterhuis, joint second in 1982 at Royal Troon.

1982 Carrolls Irish Open at Portmarnock was nothing less than his commitment to the game deserved. He was on the Ryder Cup team in 1975, and won a handful of events, but a place among the true superstars has eluded him so far.

Peter Oosterhuis *Twice runner-up in the Open – in 1974 and 1982 – he was top of the Order of Merit from 1971 to 1974. He looked for a new challenge by going full-time on the US tour but his victory in the 1981 Canadian Open remains the only oasis in a desert of disappointments. Even so, he has served Great Britain and Ireland well in the Ryder Cup.*

Philip Parkin *Turned professional on 3 July 1984, then teed up in the Open at St Andrews. A closing 69 gave him 31st place and provided concrete evidence that, following an excellent start to his golfing career in which he won the 1983 Amateur Championship, he will develop into a multi-winner. He was named 'rookie of the year' in 1984 and had four top-ten finishes in 1985.*

Ronan Rafferty *An up-and-coming golfer who possesses a touch of class. He won the Venezuelan Open in 1982, shortly after turning professional, and gained valuable experience at St Andrews in 1984 by finishing joint eighth in the Open. He climbed to 17th in the Order of Merit in 1985, gaining no less than nine top-ten finishes, then began 1986 the way he had left off the previous season. An aggressive player who accepts that more experience could provide the right ammunition for him to climb to lofty heights.*

José Rivero *The slim Spaniard did not disappoint Tony Jacklin, who selected him for the 1985 Ryder Cup at The Belfry, when he teamed-up with José-María Cañizares to thrash Tom Kite and Calvin Peete 7 and 5*

in the foursomes. It was at The Belfry again in 1984 that he won the Lawrence Batley International. He also paired up with Cañizares to win the World Cup for Spain in Rome in 1984.

David J Russell *Broke through, after twelve years as a professional, by winning the Car Care Plan International at Moortown in 1985. With the confidence derived from that success he should achieve more conquests, as he possesses the happy knack of producing astonishing bursts of scoring.*

Ove Sellberg *Took the Swedish nation to the top of the professional tree for the first time when he won the Epson Grand Prix by beating Howard Clark in the final at St Pierre, Chepstow, in 1986. He has learned his trade well and he gave an indication of his prowess by finishing joint second in the Ebel European Masters in 1985.*

Des Smyth *A popular Irishman, he was regarded as the best putter*

among the British and Irish players when he finished joint fourth in the 1982 Open. He subsequently lost faith in that implement and found it difficult to maintain the momentum of a career highlighted by five victories between 1979 and 1983, including the European Match-Play Championship. But he returned to form in 1986 when he was edged out in a play-off by Australian Rodger Davis for the Whyte and Mackay PGA Championship at Wentworth.

Brian Waites *A prime example that golf is not just a young man's game, Brian did not compete regularly on the European tour until 1978, when he was in his 38th year, but since then has won no less than seven tournaments. He gained universal recognition by making the European Ryder Cup team in 1983.*

Below Ove Sellberg claims victory in the 1986 Epson Grand Prix of Europe – the first time that a Swedish golfer has won on the European tour.

SUNNINGDALE

Swinging round the Walker Cup venue

Because of statements made by some of the professionals there are probably a lot of people who believe that the Old course at Sunningdale is easy. Some professionals have even made out a case that this is one of the courses on which a 59 can be shot. But the subtlety of the greens often restricts low scoring, even if you play very well and create a lot of chances. It is a course, however, where a professional will want to be four to six under par if he is playing well. The key is in reading the hidden undulations on greens which are generally extremely fast. In fact, some of the best inland greens in England are to be found at Sunningdale. The bottom line is that the Old course is a little tougher than it would appear to be at first sight . . . a little like Augusta, in that there are hidden qualities with holes that must be played up the correct side of the fairway to provide the best shot into the green. If you do all that, then you will be rewarded.

Hole 1: A fairly straightforward par five, which offers the chance of a good start as it can be reached with a driver and a long iron. Round the green everything runs from right to left into the green – so the bunkers front and left should not be a problem. A 'must' birdie hole.

Hole 2: A dog-leg left, where it is imperative to draw the tee shot round the corner, over the road. Then you have a downhill shot which is semi-

blind – you usually just see the top of the flag – to a green that slopes quite a bit from front to back and is generally quite quick. This is always a tricky hole where it is not too hard to drop a shot. It normally plays quite long – a driver and a long iron.

Hole 3: A shortish par four, which a lot of players can drive, especially in the summer months, although it is guarded by a multitude of traps down the right and around the green. It is a birdie chance and, with nothing to worry about in front of the green, a good tee shot will leave a reasonably easy pitch. The green slopes left to right with a couple of funny little ridges on which they can 'hide' the pin.

Hole 4: A good par three up the hill, this usually requires a mid-iron, anywhere between 5 and 7, but once again the green slopes severely from the front to the back. It is also guarded by a deep trap on the front

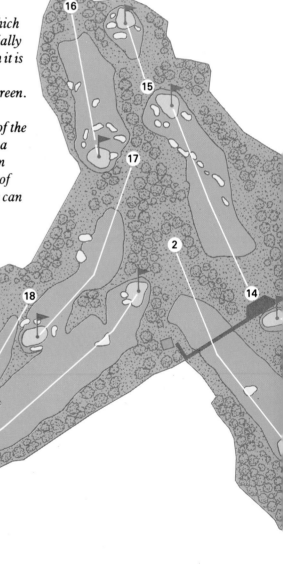

left. *The green is almost a plateau, perched on the side of a hill so that it falls off down the right towards the heather and the sand paths. A good shot is rewarded but if you hit it past the hole then you leave yourself a very quick putt back.*

Hole 5: *You tee off here from an elevated tee down into a valley, with the fairway a considerable distance below you, with two bunkers down the right-hand side. Generally, most*

ARD OF THE COURSE		
OUT		
HOLE	YARDS	PAR
1	494	5
2	484	5
3	296	4
4	161	3
5	410	4
6	415	4
7	402	4
8	172	3
9	267	4
	3101	36

IN		
HOLE	YARDS	PAR
10	478	5
11	325	4
12	451	4
13	185	3
14	509	5
15	226	3
16	438	4
17	421	4
18	432	4
	3465	36
TOTAL	6566	72

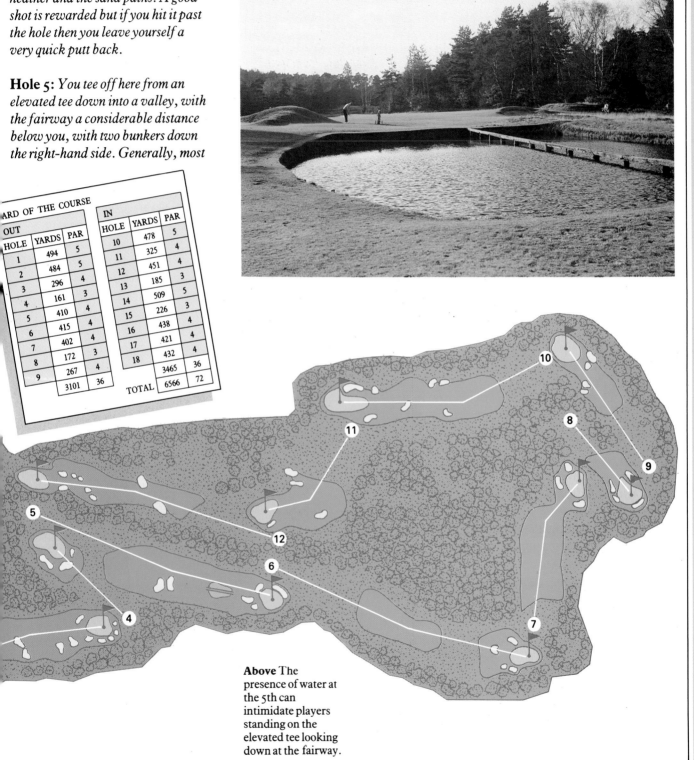

Above The presence of water at the 5th can intimidate players standing on the elevated tee looking down at the fairway.

Above The second shot to the 7th is one of the prettiest in golf but you will be punished if you miss the green.

of the professionals will hit a 1-iron or a 3-wood about level with those bunkers, leaving themselves a medium iron into the green. The hole does narrow so you must also beware of the heather on the left. You can't smash a driver, because if you really caught it the ball would end up in a pond. The green slopes front to back and slightly left to right, so once again it's quite a tricky second shot, often made more difficult by the wind.

Hole 6: Driving to an island fairway which, off the back tee, starts at about 180 yards then runs out at about 280 yards, you usually need a 3-wood again. The second shot, however, is played uphill and plays longer than it looks, especially with a deceptive breeze coming over the top of the trees. The green slopes again, from back to front, and drops off on the right-hand side and round the back to the tune of about six or seven feet. The hole plays something like a 3-wood and a 5-iron – depending on how brave you feel, hitting it towards the end of the fairway.

Hole 7: The drive here is over a massive mound. It's probably best to take a 3-wood again as the fairway has a hollow in it and the idea is to hit the ball on to the top of the second ridge. But you don't want to go too far because the ball will run all the way down and leave you blocked out behind fir trees. There is a blind tee-shot so it's not an easy strike. The second shot is probably one of the prettiest in English golf, to a green on the side of the hill. There are very steep bunkers on the left side, where the land falls away. The green, which is guarded on the right side by thick heather and a few gorse bushes, is relatively fair – but if you miss it, then you will normally be penalized.

Hole 8: Another tricky par three, basically because of the swirling wind one normally gets there. The green slopes severely from left to right so anything top-side is very, very quick. There's a deep bunker front right, set halfway down the embankment, and another that runs around the left towards the back of the green. It's a good hole which requires a very well placed tee shot.

Hole 9: A driveable par four, but if you miss it back left then the ball usually runs all the way down a slope towards the ladies' tee of the tenth. A relatively new tier had been put into the green, running from front to back up the right side of the putting surface. Generally, most of the players can knock it on with a 3-wood . . . but it's such an easy hole that you become infuriated if you mess it up. It's not one of my favourites!

Hole 10: You set off from a high, elevated tee here, which looks out over the whole of the forest. Driving down the hill, missing a couple of bunkers down the right and one down the left, leaves a relatively long second shot ranging from a 4-iron to even a 3-wood. Once again the green has a severe slope running through the middle, left to right. The front right corner of the green is guarded by a big trap. But the main feature here is the halfway hut, where the famous sausage-in-brown-bread and hot Bovril is served!

Hole 11: A very tricky blind tee-shot over a mound. Once again, distance is not required – you hit a long iron or a 3-wood – and there is a water hazard down the right side. The main secret really is not to drive it too far, because there is a bunker front left and if they put the pin behind that it's almost impossible to stop the ball close to the hole. It's quite a testing hole, and the pitch requires a bit of variation. As often as not you can be playing a delicate pitch and run – landing the ball short of the green and hoping to bounce it over the first little ridge on the front of the very small green. If you've got the right distance to go, then you can play a full sand wedge and get a lot of backspin to stop the ball.

Hole 12: *This is a nice hole. There is a bunker down the left, which the pros can carry, but another on the right at about 245 yards which comes into play if you mishit it. The hole is a slight dog-leg left, moving uphill to a plateau green with gorse banks around it. The green is very undulating, with lots of contours that don't really go anywhere so you must hit the approach on to the correct side of the hole.*

Hole 13: *From an elevated tee, which knocks a club and a half off the distance so that it plays a lot shorter than the yardage, you fire down the hill. The swirling wind also complicates club selection. Even so, I believe there is a good possibility of making two here.*

Hole 14: *Another potential birdie hole. It turns slightly, left to right, after the drive. You drive for the corner of the big trap down the right side and if you've done that then you can normally reach the green, which has nothing in front of it to worry about. The second shot, if struck well, will bounce up the green. You are hitting the second shot over a few traps and the green is relatively flat, so it does give you the chance to make a putt.*

Hole 15: *A testing par three. It often requires a 1- or 2-iron. Quite frankly it's not a very exciting hole. It has a big trap down the left-hand side and a ridge down the right, so it's really just a case of trying to hit an accurate shot. This hole probably gets you more on sheer length. The green is reasonably fair – but if you are trying to force a shot there, then it's not too difficult to pull the ball into that left trap.*

Hole 16: *This has a nice, generous fairway. There are a couple of bunkers down the right-hand side but these should not be a problem. The second shot is half-blind and uphill, so it always plays further than it looks – and further than you think. The problem is that although you can see the brow of the hill, there is another 20 yards after that of 'hidden ground' to a flattish green guarded front left by a trap. The problem there is believing you need more club to get up the hill and on to the green.*

Hole 17: *A dog-leg to the right down the hill, with bunkers on the*

right and a dangerous copse of fir trees down the left, which can very easily block you out. The correct shot, then, is to hit an iron and hang back on the hill. There is another route, if you are feeling very brave, which is to take the driver and go down the right seeking to clear everything. The penalties are quite considerable if you miss! The green is quite big, sloping left to right – but a gorse and heather bunker down the left side, and sand bunkers on the right, guard it quite nicely.*

Hole 18: *This has a bunker halfway up the left-hand side. The ideal line is to go up the left-hand side, because it gives you a better view into the green, especially as there are some very thick gorse bushes and heather plus a large trap on the right. The hole once again plays longer than it looks and the green is well guarded. It is a good finishing hole – and you putt out, of course, underneath the world famous oak tree.*

Below The dog-legged 17th can be overpowered by taking a driver but a wayward tee shot is heavily penalized.

might meet during the final round of an Open Championship. Even so there is usually an interesting mix of thoroughbred amateur and prospective professional whose approaches to the game complement each other and make for a determined team.

Michael Bonallack, now secretary of the Royal and Ancient, missed not a single Walker Cup from 1957 to 1973 during which time he won the Amateur Championship on no less than five occasions. He says: 'If anyone thinks that golf is a selfish game, let him experience the thrill of taking part in a Walker Cup match. He would soon learn that there is more team spirit between players in this seemingly slow-moving game than in many of the action-packed team games. At golf a player is acutely aware of the pressures which are affecting his partner in a foursome, or even a fellow team member in another game, and it is this mutual understanding of the pressures involved that can be of tremendous help to a player at a crucial time.'

And if one measures pressure in terms of prestige then there is as much pressure on the Walker Cup players as there is on their Ryder Cup counterparts. The Walker Cup, too, had very similar beginnings to those of the Ryder Cup as it was started by an informal match on the eve of the Amateur Championship at Royal Liverpool in 1921. The first official match took place in America the following year so that from that time the twin targets of the conventional amateur were to win the Amateur Championship and play in the Walker Cup match. The Amateur, of course, remains the more difficult to attain, especially in an era such as that dominated in his time by Bonallack, whereas the Walker Cup is played every two years with each team comprising ten players, although only eight play at any one time.

Soon after the start of the Walker Cup it was clear that the times they were a-changing when the great British golfer Harold Hilton confessed: 'To put the matter in the very plainest of language, American players of the present day are better golfers than their British cousins.'

The Walker Cup has become a true reflection of those words although Great Britain and Ireland have had their moments before contriving to snatch defeat from the jaws of victory. For instance in the 1965 match, at Baltimore, Great Britain and Ireland led 10-5 moving into the eight singles of which they were required to win only two to complete a historic win. It was time to thumb through the record books as Great Britain and Ireland prepared for only their second Walker Cup win and their first since St Andrews in 1938.

It was not to be. The Americans

Left Michael Bonallack (left) outside the clubhouse of the Royal and Ancient at St Andrews of which he is Club Secretary. With him is the 1983-4 captain, John Salvesen.

Right The clubhouse at Royal Birkdale, which was the venue for the 1969 Ryder Cup match.

won six of the singles and halved another so that the match was tied and Great Britain and Ireland had to wait for St Andrews in 1971 to record their second victory.

If there is to be another victory on home soil in 1987 then it will be historic since the Walker Cup is moving to Sunningdale. So for the first time since the late George Walker, president in 1920 of the United States Golf Association,

Above The Eden estuary and the Old course at St Andrews – the venue for the Walker Cup eight times since 1923.

donated the Walker Cup, the match is being played on an inland course. The tradition has been to take the Walker Cup, like the Open Championship, to links courses and it has been played at St Andrews on no fewer than eight occasions.

The Royal and Ancient, however, announced at a similar time that in 1987 the Amateur Championship would be staged at Prestwick, where it has not been played since 1952 and where the Open Championship was first played in 1860. There are those who have classified Prestwick as a museum piece but the important point is that, in spite of all the blind shots over massive dunes, it is a good course for match play.

FALDO ON PUTTING

'You drive for show and putt for dough.' This saying may have been around for a long time but it still applies all the same. What good is it to split every fairway with a drive of power and precision, and fire a searing iron shot to stop four feet from the hole if the putt is going to miss? Yet even today, and in spite of constant reminders from professionals, most amateur golfers still seem intent on dismissing the importance of practising on the putting green.

So how do you avoid regularly taking three putts to finish a hole – thereby handing your opponent an advantage – and consequently paying up at the bar after a 'friendly' two-ball? The key to success is: be brave. It does not matter what putter you have – that is down to personal preference – but it does matter that you take a positive stance and make a decisive stroke. If, for instance, you are 40 feet from the hole and you leave the ball five feet short then the chances are that

The stance – showing the eyes, the hole and the ball in a straight line

Position of the feet in relation to the ball for putting

you will miss the following putt because you have not given yourself the opportunity to learn the

topography of the ground that remains between you and the hole. But if you are filled with good

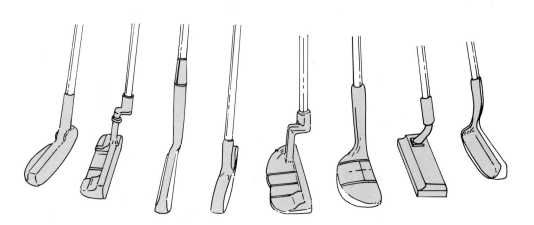

The style of a putter's head is solely a matter of the player's preference

Far right Assess the putt, take a positive stance and make a decisive stroke.

Sam Snead's unique putting stance.

intention, and you strike a solid and authoritative putt, then even if the ball misses the hole, it will most probably have travelled past and provided you with the chance to study the likely route for your next attempt to hole out.

One of the best methods to learn to be positive is to play yourself on the putting green. Take three balls, a number one, two and three, from your bag and pretend that you are playing Seve Ballesteros and Nick Faldo. I remember the Australian Ian Baker-Finch, who challenged for the Open at St Andrews in the summer of 1984, saying that he did something similar as a youngster . . . and that he took on Jack Nicklaus and Tom Watson and always won! Basically it's a question of learning to compete, learning that to be

successful at putting is not simply a question of meeting the two essentials – a balanced stance and a motionless head and body – but more a question of being brave so that the ball always has a chance of going in.

Now one thing that you can learn on the practice green before going out is the pace you can expect to face on the greens on the course. Time spent on the practice green will provide a good indication although you must learn certain aspects of the greens which, if interpreted correctly, will tell you a good deal more. For instance you can learn to feel, through the soles of your golf shoes, the texture of the greens. Whether they are hard or soft, dry or wet, will provide the basis for solving the ever-present riddle of how hard to hit the putt. Look at the colour of the grass:

The stance for putting – feet comfortably apart and the ball nearer to the toe of the left shoe

The backswing – the putter is taken back low and smooth, and the head is not moved

Just after contact – the ball has been hit cleanly and the head is still not moved

if it is light, and turning brown, then the greens are going to be on the quick side, but if it is bottle-green, then expect them to be very slow.

Of course, the pace of a putt will depend on whether it is uphill or downhill but it will also be determined by the direction of the grain – in other words, the way the grass is growing. If the grass is growing downhill on a downhill putt then you are facing a real knee-knocking putt – one that you will do well to get close to the hole even from a distance of 12 feet. Remember, too, that the ball will obey the grain so that a break which, according to the contour of the green, would appear to be two inches can become twice that much if the grass is growing in the same direction as the break.

Gary Player, consistently one of the world's best on the putting greens, uses his putter to line up his shot for the hole.

In certain countries the grain can be so strong, as in South Africa where at times the grass seems like plastic and you can virtually hear the grass pushing up from beneath your feet, that even a three-foot putt can have such a sharp break that you become apprehensive. I remember one golfer telling me out there that he was walking up a green and the grain of the grass was so strong that he was momentarily thrown off-balance and almost fell into a bunker.

Of course, the grain is not so strong on most British courses but nevertheless it is important to understand the way a putt is going to move. One of the aspects of putting that few people seem to practise is reading those breaks. So when you are on the putting green remember not to simply hit putt after putt at the hole – take a look at the line first, hit the ball on different lines and watch. You will get a feedback that will help you make those teasing four-and five-footers every time . . . and assist you in getting the ball close from long range.

Putting on sloping ground

point at which the ball begins to break

direction of aim

The follow-through – the eyes continue to look down, the upper trunk pivots slightly and the player only looks up when the ball is well on its way

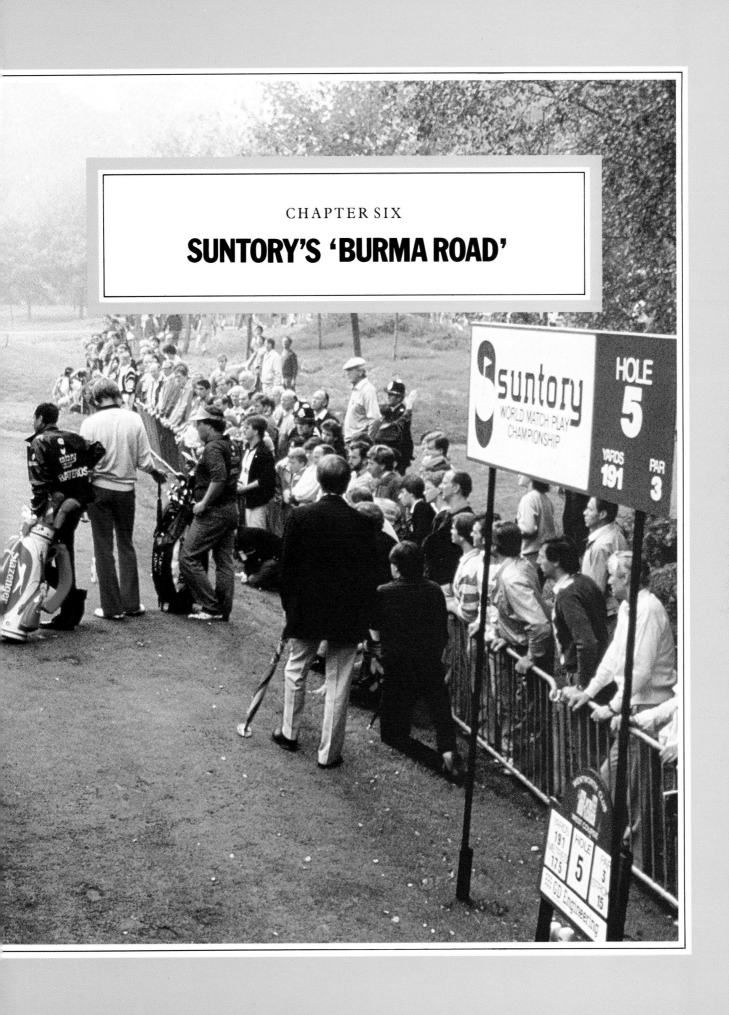

CHAPTER SIX

SUNTORY'S 'BURMA ROAD'

CHAPTER SIX

SUNTORY'S 'BURMA ROAD' –

the World Match-Play Championship

'Who are you burying?' asked Arnold Palmer, eyeing the deadpan faces of the world's golfing press. 'It looks like a funeral home in here.'

The place? Wentworth. The scene? The giant interview room where the golfing scribes gather to conduct post-round autopsies. The situation? Palmer, golf's greatest gladiator, had been ruthlessly cut down, when victory seemed assured, by Severiano Ballesteros.

Since its inception in 1964 the World Match-Play Championship, initially sponsored by Piccadilly then by Colgate and now by Suntory, has generated moments of magic to be constantly recalled rather than infrequently lifted

down and dusted from some golfing archives. But in 1983 – as if to celebrate the Championship's 20th contestation – there was a match which, ages before the contenders stepped on the first tee, was to guarantee the audience a memorable encounter.

Palmer, golf's king of entertainment in the Swinging Sixties, was back topping the bill in a head-to-head confrontation with Ballesteros. And the fans – a record 13,350 – packed the fairways to watch yesterday's favourite tackle today's hero. The American held no illusions about his task. Palmer, aged 54, was giving Seve 28 years. 'I'm a grandfather,' he chortled. 'I've got a daughter back home

older than Seve.'

About the only thing in Palmer's favour was that the issue would be decided over 18 holes. The sponsors and the organizers had no option because, by offering places to all past champions to celebrate the event, they had increased the field, but the number of daylight hours precluded the first round being played to the usual 36 holes.

Ballesteros started a hot favourite but he would have been even hotter if the match had been scheduled to go the full distance, as that would have tested Palmer's stamina on the energy-sapping Wentworth course known universally as the 'Burma Road'.

Instead Palmer teed off in the

Previous spread
Seve Ballesteros on his way to yet another Suntory World Match-Play Championship victory. He has succeeded four times to date.

Right The clubhouse at Wentworth.

Above Arnold Palmer competing in the World Match-Play Championship, Wentworth, 1965.

knowledge that if he made a fast start he might give the young 'whipper-snapper' something to think about as the real estate ran out. Moreover, match play suited the implacable Palmer. Go-for-broke golfers like Arnold can squeeze success from impending failure. So even now, with the 'Go Arnie, Go' signs a relic of the past, he was prepared to have a bash on behalf of those remaining from his faithful British 'Army'.

Palmer remembered too that as a kid he had faced a legendary opponent, Sam Snead, in a series of

'This is one of the most important tournaments in the world. I think the Americans would be advised to play more head-to-head golf – remember the Europeans are getting the swing of things in the Ryder Cup.'

Severiano Ballesteros on the World Match-Play Championship

seven head-to-head duels and that he had been regarded as odds-on favourite. Palmer was thrashed: he won only two of the seven matches against the cock-a-hoop Snead.

At Wentworth it was Palmer who was cock-a-hoop – for 17 holes and two shots. Two up, with two to play, he lost the 17th but the 18th appeared well within his grip. Palmer, on the edge of the green in three, was looking for a half to retain his lead and, with Ballesteros

Left Seve Ballesteros at the 7th at Wentworth.

167

60 yards short of the hole in two, he appeared in good shape.

Then the phenomenon that is Severiano Ballesteros struck. He didn't just chip the ball close – he chipped it straight into the hole. And, three extra holes later, Ballesteros was the victor and Palmer the vanquished. Thus Palmer entered the press tent. Was Seve lucky at the 18th? 'No,' stated Arnie, categorically. 'When I was younger, and I was making those

Left Seve Ballesteros has only been surpassed in the World Match-Play by Gary Player who has recorded five wins. **Below** The 18th green at Wentworth.

shots, I used to think they were just good shots.'

Does the word 'luck', then, enter into golf? Gary Player, who dominated the first four years of the World Match-Play Championship with Palmer and went on to win the title a record five times, perpetually insists: 'It's strange, but the harder I work the luckier I seem to get.' Gary has a politician's knack of being capable of diplomatically parrying verbal thrusts but, at the same time, he is prepared to voice his view if he feels that somebody is stepping out of line.

In the second World Match-Play

Left Tony Lema drives off at the 17th at Wentworth during the 1965 World Match-Play Championship. During the semi-final, Lema built up a 7-stroke lead, only to lose to Gary Player.

Below Gary Player urges a putt home during the 1969 World Match-Play Championship at Wentworth.

Championship, in 1965, Player took part in what is still regarded as the most astonishing recovery in the history of the championship. But a clue to his comeback was his reaction to the audible remarks of a certain spectator who chastised Player's match for its lack of interest.

Quite simply Tony Lema, who had won the Open Championship the previous year, had set Wentworth alight with a spectacular scoring spree on the inward half of the first 18 holes and with the assistance of six birdies the American lunched in the clubhouse with a commanding six-hole advantage over a disconsolate Player. Moreover, Lema won the first hole in the afternoon to extend his lead to seven with 17 to play. It was on the way to the next tee that Player overheard a spectator insisting to a friend that they should move off and watch Palmer

who was involved in a stirring battle with the Australian Peter Thomson.

Player swung round on his feet and he politely rebuked the spectator. What happened next is history. Player won three of the

next four holes – four down. He lost the sixth and, with nine to play, he was still five down. But wins at the 10th and 11th reduced the deficit to three. Then, after Lema had holed from 30 feet after being in trouble at the 13th, Player

GLENEAGLES

The well-designed King's course is set in hilly moorland and offers an unrelenting test of golfing skills.

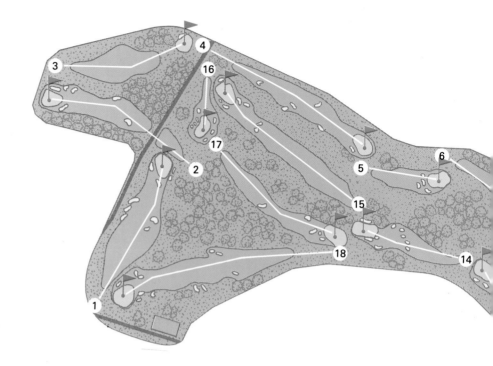

Below The Dormy House – the clubhouse at Gleneagles.

Right and below A pictorial study of Gleneagles showing the beauty of the surrounding area and the majesty of the world famous Gleneagles hotel, set amidst typical Highland scenery.

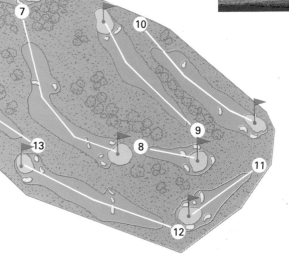

CARD OF THE COURSE

OUT					IN			
HOLE	NAME	YARDS	PAR					
1	Dun Whinny	362	4		HOLE	NAME	YARDS	PAR
2	East Neuk	405	4		10	Canty Lye	445	4
3	Silver Tassie	377	4		11	Deil's Creel	230	3
4	Broomy Law	465	4		12	Tappit Hen	387	4
5	Het Girdle	160	3		13	Braid's Brawest	446	4
6	Blink Bonnie	476	5		14	Denty Den	260	4
7	Kittle Kink	439	4		15	Howe o' Hope	457	4
8	Whaup's Nest	158	3		16	Wee Bogle	133	3
9	Heich o' Fash	351	4		17	Warslin' Lea	376	4
		3193	35		18	King's Hame	525	5
							3259	35
						TOTAL	6452	70

rammed home a ten-footer. He was two down – then it was one as Lema came off second best after an argument with the Wentworth trees at the 16th.

Who now could dare to watch? The atmosphere was electric. Player, cocooned in concentration, felt so intense that he was no longer aware of the crowd, and Lema, feeling so forlorn, was frustrated by the erosion of what had appeared an unassailable advantage.

The par five 17th – the 35th hole in all – was halved so Player, still one behind, was required to follow a majestic drive at the 18th with a

Right Gay Brewer found Gary Player too hot to handle in the World Match-Play Championship in 1967.

'It is the raw blood and guts of golf. It's one man against one man. The thrill of coming from behind to win can leave you in ecstasy . . . but at the same time physically and mentally drained.'

Gary Player on match-play golf

second shot of around 240 yards which demanded both precision and power. He virtually swung himself off his feet as he ripped a 4-wood through the ball which came to rest no more than ten feet from the hole, so that the South African forced this incredible confrontation into extra time.

When Player won at the first extra hole he fainted and had to be helped back to the clubhouse, while Lema left the course in a state of shock. But, whatever the condition of the two players, the match had positively proved one

point: the World Match-Play Championship was here to stay.

Player, of course, has become the hero of the Championship. He has been involved in countless stirring confrontations and, although it was Palmer who returned to win in 1967, it was Player who lit the blue touch-paper on another extraordinary week. In the quarter finals he was level with Gay Brewer, then the US Masters champion, when he holed a 75-foot putt for an eagle at the 35th hole which left his American opponent wearing a look of total disbelief.

TOM WEISKOPF

The 'swing's the thing' with Weiskopf, whose most ardent admirers have been his fellow professionals. At his peak, he was generally recognized as having the finest swing in golf and that smooth, predictable action led him to achieve his greatest triumph – the Open Championship at Troon in 1973. He splashed through torrential rain to beat Johnny Miller, his victory carrying a double-edged satisfaction as he had finally silenced the critics who claimed his temperament was suspect under pressure and had also emerged from the shadow of golf's Golden Bear – Jack Nicklaus. Weiskopf, born November 9 1942, in Massillon, Ohio, had always found it hard to accept comparisons with Nicklaus, Ohio's favourite son.

The Open title contributed to Weiskopf's most successful season in a tournament career which began in 1965 and ended in 1984. In addition to the Open, he won the World Series of Golf and the South African PGA and banked 245,463 dollars from the US circuit that year. He has twice represented the United States in the Ryder Cup against Great Britain and Ireland and is also remembered for 15 US Tour wins. But his graveyard proved to be Augusta where the 6ft 3in golfer finished runner-up four times

in the US Masters. Weiskopf then turned his back on tournament golf but is still an integral part of the game, switching his attention to course design and TV commentating. His 19 years of tournament combat yielded career earnings of nearly two and a quarter million dollars. Weiskopf's other wins outside the United States included the 1972 Piccadilly World Match-Play at Wentworth and the Benson and Hedges International at Fulford, York.

Right Tom Weiskopf – a hero in his time.

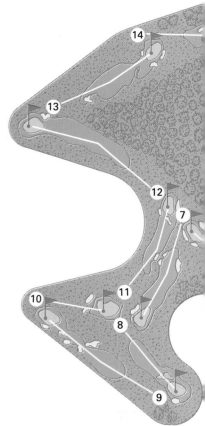

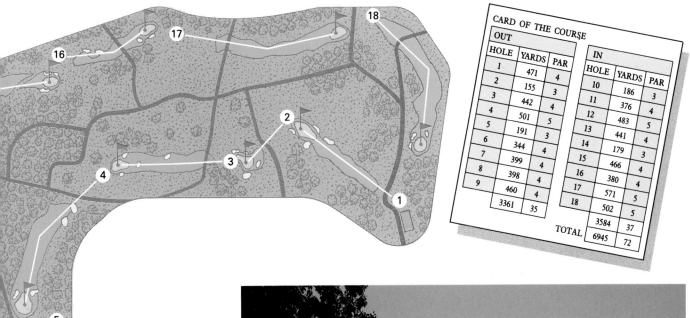

CARD OF THE COURSE						
OUT				**IN**		
HOLE	YARDS	PAR		HOLE	YARDS	PAR
1	471	4		10	186	3
2	155	3		11	376	4
3	442	4		12	483	5
4	501	5		13	441	4
5	191	3		14	179	3
6	344	4		15	466	4
7	399	4		16	380	4
8	398	4		17	571	5
9	460	4		18	502	5
	3361	35			3584	37
			TOTAL		6945	72

WENTWORTH

Home of the Suntory
World Match-Play
Championship, the West
course is set in rolling
woodland and rewards long
and accurately-placed tee
shots.

Above left
Bernhard Langer
crosses to the 8th
green during the
1984 World Match-
Play.

Left Sandy Lyle
tees off against
Severiano
Ballesteros at the
start of the Suntory
World Match-Play
Championship.

Right Wentworth
was the venue of the
second informal
match in 1926.
Once more, the
Americans were
soundly beaten.

Brewer, to his credit, countered with a winning 11-footer at the 36th, sending the match into extra time, and, after watching Player hole from six feet to stay alive at the 38th, the chubby-faced American sparked another Wentworth controversy.

Peering through the rain towards the third, or 39th, green he insisted: 'That flag isn't where it was earlier. What's going on?' The answer was quite simple. The greenkeeper had already cut a new hole for the semi-final the following day. Brewer ordered, as was his

right, the old hole to be brought back into play although, sadly for him, it made no difference. He slammed a 4-wood into a greenside bunker and Player required no more assistance.

Player and Palmer dominated the event in the first five years, before the likes of Jack Nicklaus, Tom Weiskopf, Bob Charles, Hale Irwin, David Graham, Graham Marsh and Isao Aoki enjoyed their moments of success, but, with the advent of the 1980s, so Seve Ballesteros and Greg Norman took control.

Both Sandy Lyle and Nick Faldo made valiant efforts but the Championship has been cruel to British challengers with Neil Coles losing to Palmer in the first final in 1964 then Tony Jacklin's hopes of victory being dashed amidst astonishing scenes in 1968.

Once again Player figured in a heated moment. The semi-final between these two determined battlers remained all square after 36 holes but with dusk falling the South African refused to continue. Torrential rain removed the prospect of play the following day so it was not until the Sunday that they resumed their contest.

Jacklin's strong drive followed by an equally impressive 1-iron put him on the green in two. Player, having missed the green, chipped his third to 12 feet. When he struck his putt he turned towards a group of spectators and accused them of shouting 'Miss it'. But the putt toppled in and Jacklin, after waiting for the commotion to die down, eventually three-putted to go down.

Jacklin was in the semi-finals again in 1972. By a coincidence he came up against Lee Trevino who, only three months earlier, had snatched the Open Championship from the British hero by dramatically chipping in at the penultimate hole at Muirfield. Trevino, four up at lunch, seemed to be coasting to another win.

Jacklin, however, responded to the crowd's encouragement after the break. He eagled two and birdied three of six holes from the fourth to move ahead. But Trevino, back to all square at the last, cut Jacklin down again with a superb

Left Lee Trevino was twice pipped at the post in the World Match-Play Championship – by Nicklaus in 1970 and Weiskopf in 1972.

HALE IRWIN

Hale Irwin has the reputation of one of the game's most brilliant shot-makers and endorsed that acclaim with Britain's golf fans in the World Match-Play Championship at Wentworth in 1974 and 1975. He won both thanks largely to uncanny accuracy with his fairway woods, beating Gary Player at the 40th hole and following with a 4 and 2 over fellow American Al Geiberger. He had already won the US Open in 1974 and took that title again in 1979, but the bespectacled Irwin, born in 1945 at Joplin, Missouri, has experienced both ends of the golfing spectrum.

He was labelled 'Mr Consistency' in 1978 after making every 36-hole cut for four years on the US Tour, covering 86 events. Only two other players in the history of the American professional circuit have bettered that performance, but the vagaries of golf were amplified when Irwin went 20 months without a victory in 1981. He said: 'It hurt my pride. You have to tell yourself that you are not immortal. You're not sitting on Zeus' throne. But while you are up there, you can really believe you are sitting there and it's a great feeling.' Irwin swiftly resumed his place 'among the gods' by collecting the Hawaiian Open and the Buick Open.

He has mounted the winner's rostrum 17 times on the US PGA Tour, the only occasion in 1985 being at the Memorial Tournament on Jack Nicklaus's Muirfield Village course (see page 144). 'The Memorial was the highlight of the year for me,' says Irwin. 'But it wasn't a banner year overall. I'm still hopeful of keeping my game together with a sharp competitive edge after 17 years on the Tour.'

That razor-sharp edge has brought him winnings of nearly three million dollars since he came through the qualifying school in the spring of 1968.

Above and right Hale Irwin won the Suntory World Match-Play in 1974 and 1975, though he never found the winning touch in the British Open.

3-wood which left the ball just eight feet from the hole.

In fact that dog-legged 18th hole has, through the regular coverage of the championship by television, become one of the most famous in the country because of the number of nail-biting tussles which have been decided there. In fact Wentworth's West course – the club has another called the East – has been the permanent venue for this classic championship although its future was in jeopardy during the Second World War when the course was allowed to run wild because of lack of funds.

The rambling clubhouse, once the home of Lady Anne Wesley, the Duke of Wellington's sister, was requisitioned as the refuge where the Chief of the Imperial General Staff could carry on the War in the event of serious problems at headquarters in London. Tunnels, some 45 feet deep, were dug under the clubhouse and the excavated material coupled with trip wires and the like were utilized to create barriers aimed at stopping the

Below Nick Faldo still seeks success in the World Match-

Play. He was runner-up to Greg Norman in 1983.

enemy from parachuting on to the fairways.

It continued the colourful history of the place since in the 1850s the house had been bought by Spanish bandit leader and exile General Ramón Cabrera who became an English gentleman. It was after his death that his wife, the Countess de Morella, purchased much of the land which is now part of the 1,750-acre estate.

The rebirth of Wentworth was launched when Major Rawlinson, then the secretary, contacted the commandant of the local prisoner-of-war camp in Egham, soon after the end of the War, and requested that a group of men be sent along to help clear the fairways which were overgrown with trees, sprouting bushes and savannah-like grass. One member voiced the opinion that as the prisoners went to work it was like seeing the Burma Road being built all over again and thus the nickname for the West course was born.

Now the 'Burma Road' is recognized as one of the most formidable inland-course examinations in Britain, starting with the 471-yard first where to reach in two the well-bunkered

green, fronted by a deep ravine, is in itself a true test for the finest golfers in the land.

The short second provided a magical moment in 1978 when Isao Aoki, of Japan, holed in one with a 7-iron for which he received a special prize of a £55,000 house at Gleneagles. It was then the biggest hole-in-one prize ever.

The third, measuring 452 yards from the championship tee, is regarded by many observers as the toughest hole on the course. A bunker on the right eats into the fairway, so the drive must be both long and precise, and the steeply tiered green is a tricky target particularly when the pin is set on the upper level.

A good drive at the fourth, where the line is down the left, will set up the possibility of a birdie four but the short fifth provides another stumbling block with the green being extremely well bunkered. The sixth is a relatively short par four and the seventh, also a par four, is often played with an iron from the tee. The problem with the eighth is the lake fronting a green which slopes and undulates from the right.

The ninth, at 450 yards, is a true par four. The optimum route is down the left, although this can mean flirting with the out-of-bounds line, so that the player has his best chance of seeing the green, well bunkered left and right, whilst preparing to strike the approach shot.

A group of fir trees provide the short tenth with some protection. The 11th, which dog-legs sharply to the left, is relatively straight-forward although the approach, with a short iron, over bunkers can prove deceptive. The 12th also dog-legs to the left but since it is a par five it provides the prospect of a

birdie although there is out-of-bounds to the left.

It is a good drive which opens up the green at the 13th, which again dog-legs to the left, and the 14th is regarded as a teasing short hole as the bottom of the pin, on a terraced green, is out of sight from the tee. The 15th, at 466 yards, is another par four although reasonably straightforward. Then comes the 380-yard 16th where, with the heat on, the urge to go for the driver can lead to trouble.

There are few supporters of the game who would not recognize the 17th – at 571 yards one of the finest par fives you could wish to play. It dog-legs to the left, with out-of-bounds running along that side, and, even after the perfect drive, many have been caught out by the second since the green cannot be seen.

If you are one down playing the last – a 502-yarder which dog-legs to the right – then it is essential, even though dangerous, to go for two massive blows so as to reach the green in two.

That is, of course, unless your name is Severiano Ballesteros. Arnold Palmer would tell you all about that!

Left Bill Rogers at the 1st green at Wentworth with the magnificent and historic clubhouse in the background.

Above Seve Ballesteros took the 1984 World Match-Play title by beating Bernhard Langer two and one.

179

FALDO ON MATCH-PLAY TACTICS

The basic code to follow, when going head to head with an opponent, is that you are still playing the course. In essence that means you should stick to playing your own game – variations are likely to be noted by an opponent as a sign of weakness.

Now if, for example, your opponent has driven out-of-bounds, so presenting you with a two-shot advantage on the tee, then you may become more cautious since it is unlikely that you will not be able to turn such a substantial advantage to your favour. But, at the same time, you must always play in the knowledge that your opponent can hole his next shot. The game of golf has a million stories of unlikely reversals so in your mind you must always be prepared for the improbable.

A good tip is to be fully aware that if you have the honour, in other words you have won the last hole or at the very least halved it to remain ahead, then the optimum approach is to make sure you hit the fairway with your tee shot in order to keep the pressure on your opponent. So it is often advantageous to take a 3-wood, or even a long iron, so that you are more likely to be in good shape and leave the tee free for your opponent to step up with some trepidation.

Now I respect that in a friendly, weekly head to head at the local club you will not wish to get involved in controversies over the rules of the games. But, in match-play golf, the rules are of paramount importance

and I believe it is essential for anybody who plays any sport to know and understand the rules of the game. So it is advisable to spend a little time swotting up the rules so that you can always apply them in a specific situation if it should arise.

If you are involved in a cut-and-thrust match then a knowledge of the rules is important, as, perhaps, is the ability to diagnose another player. If you have a regular opponent, you should learn his characteristics such as the pace at which he walks the fairways, how he sets up or waggles the club or, for instance, whether he talks more when he is winning. Any change in his mannerisms can be a clue to how he is feeling that day and to what shape he feels his game is in.

But it is also important to

recognize that you can pay too much attention to your opponent. This game, your game, is hard enough to understand without increasing the complications so that you momentarily forget the fundamentals which will enable you to play your best golf. And, if that is not good enough on the day, then at least your opponent should be buying the drinks after the game.

Left Nick Faldo and Peter Oosterhuis discuss the strategy to be adopted during a Ryder Cup match.

Right Nick Faldo and Bernhard Langer were a formidable fighting force in the 1983 Ryder Cup in Florida.

ISAO AOKI

They label them the 'shots heard around the world' – glory shots never to be forgotten – and the Japanese golfer had his at the Waialae Country Club in the 1983 Hawaiian Open. He was 128 yards from the hole, in knee-high rough, and he had to get down in two to tie Jack Renner. Aoki went one better – he holed out for an astonishing eagle and victory. Nicknamed the 'Tower', after the Tokyo Tower, by his former fellow caddies as he stands six feet tall. Born 31 August 1942, he turned professional in 1964 and waited seven years for his first win. Since then he has won more than 40 times including 1978 World Match-Play Championship and 1983 European Open. Runner-up to Jack Nicklaus in 1980 US Open. Holed in one to win £55,000 Bovis home during 1979 World Match-Play Championship at Wentworth and again to win £60,000 Excalibur car during Johnnie Walker Monte Carlo Open in 1985 at Mont Agel.

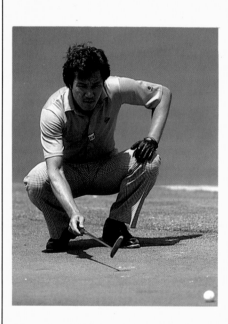

Above Isao Aoki had the very good fortune to score a hole-in-one at the 2nd at Wentworth during the 1978 World Match-Play Championship and went on to win.

Right Aoki splashes safely out of a bunker during the 1984 version of the US Masters at Augusta.

THE RESULTS –
the seven major tournaments

BRITISH OPEN CHAMPIONSHIP

The Belt

Year	Winner	Score	Runner-up	Score	Venue	Entrants
1860	Willie Park	174	Tom Morris Sr	176	Prestwick	8
	(twelve-hole course; 36 holes played in one day)					
1861	Tom Morris Sr	163	Willie Park	167	Prestwick	12
1862	Tom Morris Sr	163	Willie Park	176	Prestwick	6
1863	Willie Park	168	Tom Morris Sr	170	Prestwick	14
1864	Tom Morris Sr	167	Andrew Strath	169	Prestwick	6
1865	Andrew Strath	162	Willie Park	164	Prestwick	10
1866	Willie Park	169	David Park	171	Prestwick	12
1867	Tom Morris Sr	170	Willie Park	172	Prestwick	10
1868	Tom Morris Jr	157	Robert Andrew	159	Prestwick	10
1869	Tom Morris Jr	154	Tom Morris Sr	157	Prestwick	8
1870	Tom Morris Jr	149	Bob Kirk	161	Prestwick	17
			David Strath	161		

1871 No competition

When Tom Morris Jr won the Belt in three successive years, it became his property. The Championship was not contested for one year while a new trophy was sought. Since 1872 the present cup has been offered as the prize each year, except during the two World Wars.

The Cup

Year	Winner	Score	Runner-up	Score	Venue	Entrants
1872	Tom Morris Jr	166	David Strath	169	Prestwick	8
1873	Tom Kidd	179	Jamie Anderson	180	St Andrews	26
1874	Mungo Park	159	Tom Morris Jr	161	Musselburgh	32
1875	Willie Park	166	Bob Martin	168	Prestwick	18
1876	Bob Martin	176	David Strath	176	St Andrews	34
	(Strath refused to play off, so Martin was awarded the title)					
1877	Jamie Anderson	160	Bob Pringle	162	Musselburgh	24
1878	Jamie Anderson	157	Bob Kirk	159	Prestwick	26
1879	Jamie Anderson	169	James Allan	172	St Andrews	46
			Andrew Kirkaldy	172		
1880	Bob Ferguson	162	Peter Paxton	167	Musselburgh	30
1881	Bob Ferguson	170	Jamie Anderson	173	Prestwick	22
1882	Bob Ferguson	171	Willie Fernie	174	St Andrews	40
1883	Willie Fernie	159	Bob Ferguson	159	Musselburgh	41
	(Fernie won play-off 158 to 159)					
1884	Jack Simpson	160	Willie Fernie	164	Prestwick	30
			David Rollan	164		
1885	Bob Martin	171	Archie Simpson	172	St Andrews	51
1886	David Brown	157	Willie Campbell	159	Musselburgh	46
1887	Willie Park Jr	161	Bob Martin	162	Prestwick	36
1888	Jack Burns	171	David Anderson Jr	172	St Andrews	53
			Ben Sayers	172		
1889	Willie Park Jr	155	Andrew Kirkaldy	155	Musselburgh	42
	(Park won play-off 158 to 163)					
1890	John Ball*	164	Willie Fernie	167	Prestwick	40
			Archie Simpson	167		
1891	Hugh Kirkaldy	166	Willie Fernie	168	St Andrews	82
			Andrew Kirkaldy	168		
1892	Harold Hilton*	305	John Ball Jr*	308	Muirfield	66
			Sandy Herd	308		
			James Kirkaldy	308		

From 1892 the competition was extended to 72 holes, and entry money was imposed

Year	Winner	Score	Runner-up	Score	Venue	Entrants
1893	Willie Auchterlonie	322	Johnny Laidlay*	324	Prestwick	72
1894	J H Taylor	326	Douglas Rolland	331	Royal St George's	94
1895	J H Taylor	322	Sandy Herd	326	St Andrews	73
1896	Harry Vardon	316	J H Taylor	316	Muirfield	64
	(Vardon won play-off 157 to 161)					

*Amateur

Year	Winner	Score	Runner-up	Score	Venue	Entrants
1897	Harold Hilton*	314	James Braid	315	Hoylake	86
1898	Harry Vardon	307	Willie Park Jr	308	Prestwick	78
1899	Harry Vardon	310	Jack White	315	Royal St George's	98
1900	J H Taylor	309	Harry Vardon	317	St Andrews	81
1901	James Braid	309	Harry Vardon	312	Muirfield	101
1902	Sandy Herd	307	James Braid	308	Hoylake	112
			Harry Vardon	308		
1903	Harry Vardon	300	Tom Vardon	306	Prestwick	127
1904	Jack White	296	James Braid	297	Royal St George's	144
			J H Taylor	297		
1905	James Braid	318	Rowland Jones	323	St Andrews	152
			J H Taylor	323		
1906	James Braid	300	J H Taylor	304	Muirfield	183
1907	Arnaud Massy	312	J H Taylor	314	Hoylake	193
1908	James Braid	291	Tom Ball	299	Prestwick	180
1909	J H Taylor	295	James Braid	299	Deal	204
1910	James Braid	299	Sandy Herd	303	St Andrews	210
1911	Harry Vardon	303	Arnaud Massy	303	Royal St George's	226
	(Massy conceded at the 35th hole during the play-off. He had taken 148 for 34 holes, and Vardon's score at the 35th after holing out was 143.)					
1912	Ted Ray	295	Harry Vardon	299	Muirfield	215
1913	J H Taylor	304	Ted Ray	312	Hoylake	269
1914	Harry Vardon	306	J H Taylor	309	Prestwick	194
1915-19 No competition owing to World War I						
1920	George Duncan	303	Sandy Herd	305	Deal	190
1921	Jock Hutchison	296	Roger Wethered	296	St Andrews	158
	(Hutchison won play-off 150 to 159)					
1922	Walter Hagen	300	George Duncan	301	Royal St George's	225
1923	Arthur Havers	295	Walter Hagen	296	Royal Troon	222
1924	Walter Hagen	301	Ernest Whitcombe	302	Hoylake	277
1925	Jim Barnes	300	Archie Compston	301	Prestwick	200
			Ted Ray	301		
1926	Bobby Jones*	291	Al Watrous	293	Royal Lytham	293
1927	Bobby Jones*	285	Audrey Boomer	291	St Andrews	207
			Fred Robson	291		
1928	Walter Hagen	292	Gene Sarazen	294	Royal St George's	271
1929	Walter Hagen	292	John Farrell	298	Muirfield	242
1930	Bobby Jones*	291	Leo Diegel	293	Hoylake	296
			Macdonald Smith	293		
1931	Tommy Armour	296	José Jurado	297	Carnoustie	215
1932	Gene Sarazen	283	Macdonald Smith	288	Prince's, Sandwich	224
1933	Densmore Shute	292	Craig Wood	292	St Andrews	287
	(Shute won play-off 149 to 154)					
1934	Henry Cotton	283	Sid Brews	288	Royal St George's	312
1935	Alf Perry	283	Alf Padgham	287	Muirfield	264
1936	Alf Padgham	287	Jimmy Adams	288	Hoylake	286
1937	Henry Cotton	290	Reg Whitcombe	292	Carnoustie	258
1938	Reg Whitcombe	295	Jimmy Adams	297	Royal St George's	268
1939	Dick Burton	290	Johnny Bulla	292	St Andrews	254
1940-45 No competition owing to World War II						
1946	Sam Snead	290	Johnny Bulla	294	St Andrews	225
			Bobby Locke	294		
1947	Fred Daly	293	Reg Horne	294	Hoylake	263
			Frank Stranahan*	294		

*Amateur

BRITISH OPEN CHAMPIONSHIP (contd)

Year	Winner	Score	Runner-up	Score	Venue	Entrants
1948	Henry Cotton	284	Fred Daly	289	Muirfield	272
1949	Bobby Locke	283	Harry Bradshaw	283	Royal St	224
	(Locke won play-off 135 to 147)				George's	
1950	Bobby Locke	279	Roberto de Vicenzo	281	Royal	262
					Troon	
1951	Max Faulkner	285	Tony Cerda	287	Portrush	180
1952	Bobby Locke	287	Peter Thomson	288	Royal	275
					Lytham	
1953	Ben Hogan	282	Tony Cerda	286	Carnoustie	196
			Dai Rees	286		
			Frank Stranahan*	286		
			Peter Thomson	286		
1954	Peter Thomson	283	Bobby Locke	284	Royal	349
			Dai Rees	284	Birkdale	
			Sid Scott	284		
1955	Peter Thomson	281	Johnny Fallon	283	St Andrews	301
1956	Peter Thomson	286	Flory van Donck	289	Hoylake	360
1957	Bobby Locke	279	Peter Thomson	282	St Andrews	282
1958	Peter Thomson	278	David Thomas	278	Royal	362
					Lytham	
	(Thomson won play-off 139 to 143)					
1959	Gary Player	284	Fred Bullock	286	Muirfield	285
			Flory van Donck	286		
1960	Kel Nagle	278	Arnold Palmer	279	St Andrews	410
1961	Arnold Palmer	284	Dai Rees	285	Royal	364
					Birkdale	
1962	Arnold Palmer	276	Kel Nagle	282	Royal	379
					Troon	
1963	Bob Charles	277	Phil Rodgers	277	Royal	261
					Lytham	
1964	Tony Lema	279	Jack Nicklaus	284	St Andrews	327
1965	Peter Thomson	285	Brian Huggett	287	Royal	372
			Christy O'Connor	287	Birkdale	
1966	Jack Nicklaus	282	Doug Sanders	283	Muirfield	310
			David Thomas	283		
1967	Roberto de Vicenzo	278	Jack Nicklaus	280	Hoylake	326
1968	Gary Player	289	Bob Charles	291	Carnoustie	309
			Jack Nicklaus	291		
1969	Tony Jacklin	280	Bob Charles	282	Royal	424
					Lytham	
1970	Jack Nicklaus	283	Doug Sanders	283	St Andrews	468
	(Nicklaus won play-off 72 to 73)					
1971	Lee Trevino	278	Liang Huan Lu	279	Royal	528
					Birkdale	
1972	Lee Trevino	278	Jack Nicklaus	279	Muirfield	570
1973	Tom Weiskopf	276	Neil Coles	279	Royal	569
			Johnny Miller	279	Troon	
1974	Gary Player	282	Peter Oosterhuis	286	Royal	679
					Lytham	
1975	Tom Watson	279	Jack Newton	279	Carnoustie	629
	(Watson won play-off 71 to 72)					
1976	Johnny Miller	279	Seve Ballesteros	285	Royal	719
			Jack Nicklaus	285	Birkdale	
1977	Tom Watson	268	Jack Nicklaus	269	Turnberry	730
1978	Jack Nicklaus	281	Ben Crenshaw	283	St Andrews	788
			Ray Floyd	283		
			Tom Kite	283		
			Simon Owen	283		
1979	Seve Ballesteros	283	Ben Crenshaw	286	Royal	885
			Jack Nicklaus	286	Lytham	
1980	Tom Watson	271	Lee Trevino	275	Muirfield	994
1981	Bill Rogers	276	Bernhard Langer	280	Royal St	972
					George's	
1982	Tom Watson	284	Peter Oosterhuis	285	Royal	1121
			Nick Price	285	Troon	
1983	Tom Watson	275	Andy Bean	276	Royal	1107
			Hale Irwin	276	Birkdale	
1984	Seve Ballesteros	276	Bernhard Langer	278	St	1413
			Tom Watson	278	Andrews	
1985	Sandy Lyle	282	Payne Stewart	283	Royal St	1361
					George's	
1986	Greg Norman	280	Gordon J. Brand	285	Turnberry	1348

US OPEN CHAMPIONSHIP

Year	Winner	Score	Runner-up	Score	Venue
1895	Horace Rawlins	173	Willie Dunn	175	Newport, R.I.
1896	James Foulis	152	Horace Rawlins	155	Shinnecock Hills, N.Y.
1897	Joe Lloyd	162	Willie Anderson	163	Chicago Club, Wheaton, Ill.
1898	Fred Herd	328	Alex Smith	335	Myopia Hunt Club, Mass.

Extended to 72 holes from 1898

Year	Winner	Score	Runner-up	Score	Venue
1899	Willie Smith	315	Val Fitzjohn	326	Baltimore, Md.
			George Low	326	
			W H Way	326	
1900	Harry Vardon	313	J H Taylor	315	Chicago Club, Wheaton, Ill.
1901	Willie Anderson	331	Alex Smith	331	Myopia Hunt Club, Mass.
	(Anderson won play-off 85 to 86)				
1902	Laurie Auchterlonie	307	Stewart Gardner	313	Garden City, N.Y.
			Walter Travis*	313	
1903	Willie Anderson	307	David Brown	307	Baltusrol, N.J.
	(Anderson won play-off 82 to 84)				
1904	Willie Anderson	303	Gilbert Nicholls	308	Glen View, Ill.
1905	Willie Anderson	314	Alex Smith	316	Myopia Hunt Club, Mass.
1906	Alex Smith	295	Willie Smith	302	Onwentsia, Ill.
1907	Alec Ross	302	Gilbert Nicholls	304	Philadelphia Cricket Club, Pa
1908	Fred McLeod	322	Willie Smith	322	Myopia Hunt Club, Mass.
	(McLeod won play-off 77 to 83)				
1909	George Sargent	290	Tom McNamara	294	Englewood, N.J.
1910	Alex Smith	298	John McDermott	298	Philadelphia Cricket Club, Pa
			Macdonald Smith	298	
	(Smith won play-off 71 to 75 to 77)				
1911	John McDermott	307	Mike Brady	307	Chicago Club, Wheaton, Ill.
			George Simpson	307	
	(McDermott won play-off 80 to 82 to 85)				
1912	John McDermott	294	Tom McNamara	296	Buffalo, N.Y.
1913	Francis Ouimet*	304	Harry Vardon	304	Brookline, Mass.
			Ted Ray	304	
	(Ouimet won play-off 72 to 77 to 78)				
1914	Walter Hagen	290	Charles Evans Jr*	291	Midlothian, Ill.
1915	Jerome Travers*	297	Tom McNamara	298	Baltusrol, N.J.
1916	Charles Evans Jr*	286	Jock Hutchison	288	Minikahda, Minn.
1917-18	No competition				
1919	Walter Hagen	301	Mike Brady	301	Brae Burn, Mass.
	(Hagen won play-off 77 to 78)				
1920	Ted Ray	295	Jack Burke	296	Inverness, Ohio
			Leo Diegel	296	
			Jock Hutchison	296	
			Harry Vardon	296	
1921	Jim Barnes	289	Walter Hagen	298	Columbia, Md.
			Fred McLeod	298	
1922	Gene Sarazen	288	John Black	289	Skokie, Ill.
			Bobby Jones*	289	
1923	Bobby Jones*	296	Bobby Cruikshank	296	Inwood, N.Y.
	(Jones won play-off 76 to 78)				
1924	Cyril Walker	297	Bobby Jones*	300	Oakland Hills, Mich.
1925	Willie Macfarlane	291	Bobby Jones*	291	Worcester, Mass.
	(Macfarlane won play-off 147 to 148)				
1926	Bobby Jones*	293	Joe Turnesa	294	Scioto, Ohio
1927	Tommy Armour	301	Harry Cooper	301	Oakmont, Pa.
	(Armour won play-off 76 to 79)				
1928	Johnny Farrell	294	Bobby Jones*	294	Olympia Fields, Ill.
	(Farrell won play-off 143 to 144)				
1929	Bobby Jones*	294	Al Espinosa	294	Winged Foot, N.Y.
	(Jones won play-off 141 to 164)				
1930	Bobby Jones*	287	Macdonald Smith	289	Interlachen, Minn.
1931	Billy Burke	292	George von Elm*	292	Inverness, Ohio
	(Burke won play-offs 149 and 148 to von Elm's 149 and 149)				

*Amateur

*Amateur

Year	Winner	Score	Runner-up	Score	Venue
1932	Gene Sarazen	286	Bobby Cruickshank	289	Fresh Meadow,
			Phil Perkins	289	N.Y.
1933	Johnny Goodman*	287	Ralph Guldahl	288	North Shore, Ill.
1934	Olin Dutra	293	Gene Sarazen	294	Merion Cricket
					Club, Pa.
1935	Sam Parks	299	Jimmy Thomson	301	Oakmont, Pa.
1936	Tony Manero	282	Harry Cooper	284	Baltusrol, N.J.
1937	Ralph Guldahl	281	Sam Snead	283	Oakland Hills,
					Mich.
1938	Ralph Guldahl	284	Dick Metz	290	Cherry Hills, Col.
1939	Byron Nelson	284	Craig Wood	284	Philadelphia,
			Densmore Shute	284	Pa.

(Nelson won play-off 138 to 141; Shute was eliminated)

1940	Lawson Little	287	Gene Sarazen	287	Canterbury,
					Ohio

(Little won play-off 70 to 73)

1941	Craig Wood	284	Densmore Shute	287	Colonial, Tex.
1942-45	No competition				
1946	Lloyd Mangrum	284	Byron Nelson	284	Canterbury,
			Vic Ghezzi	284	Ohio

(Mangrum won play-offs 72 and 72 to Nelson's 72 and 73 and Ghezzi's 72 and 73)

1947	Lew Worsham	282	Sam Snead	282	St Louis, Mo.

(Worsham won play-off 69 to 70)

1948	Ben Hogan	276	Jimmy Demaret	278	Riviera, Calif.
1949	Cary Middlecoff	286	Clayton Heafner	287	Medinah, Ill.
			Sam Snead	287	
1950	Ben Hogan	287	Lloyd Mangrum	287	Merion, Pa.
			George Fazio	287	

(Hogan won play-off 69 to 73 to 75)

1951	Ben Hogan	287	Clayton Heafner	289	Oakland Hills,
					Mich.
1952	Julius Boros	281	Porky Oliver Jr	285	Northwood, Tex.
1953	Ben Hogan	283	Sam Snead	289	Oakmont, Pa.
1954	Ed Furgol	284	Gene Littler	285	Baltusrol, N.J.
1955	Jack Fleck	287	Ben Hogan	287	Olympic, Calif.

(Fleck won play-off 69 to 72)

1956	Cary Middlecoff	281	Julius Boros	282	Oak Hill, N.Y.
1957	Dick Mayer	282	Cary Middlecoff	282	Inverness, Ohio

(Mayer won play-off 72 to 79)

1958	Tommy Holt	283	Gary Player	287	Southern Hills,
					Okla.
1959	Billy Casper	282	Bob Rosburg	283	Winged Foot,
					N.Y.
1960	Arnold Palmer	280	Jack Nicklaus*	282	Cherry Hills, Col.
1961	Gene Littler	281	Bob Goalby	282	Oakland Hills,
			Doug Sanders	282	Mich.
1962	Jack Nicklaus	283	Arnold Palmer	283	Oakmont, Pa.

(Nicklaus won play-off 71 to 74)

1963	Julius Boros	293	Jacky Cupit	293	The Country
			Arnold Palmer	293	Club, Mass.

(Boros won play-off 70 to 73 to 76)

1964	Ken Venturi	278	Tommy Jacobs	282	Congressional,
					Washington, DC
1965	Gary Player	282	Kel Nagle	282	Bellerive, Mo.

(Player won play-off 71 to 74)

1966	Billy Casper	278	Arnold Palmer	278	Olympic, Calif.

(Casper won play-off 69 to 73)

1967	Jack Nicklaus	275	Arnold Palmer	279	Baltusrol, N.J.
1968	Lee Trevino	275	Jack Nicklaus	279	Oak Hill, N.Y.
1969	Orville Moody	281	Deane Beaman	282	Champions, Tex.
			Al Geiberger	282	
			Bob Rosburg	282	
1970	Tony Jacklin	281	Dave Hill	288	Hazeltine, Minn.
1971	Lee Trevino	280	Jack Nicklaus	280	Merion, Pa.

(Trevino won play-off 68 to 71)

1972	Jack Nicklaus	290	Bruce Crampton	293	Pebble Beach,
					Calif.
1973	Johnny Miller	279	John Schlee	280	Oakmont, Pa.
1974	Hale Irwin	287	Forest Fezler	289	Winged Foot,
					N.Y.

*Amateur

Year	Winner	Score	Runner-up	Score	Venue
1975	Lou Graham	287	John Mahaffey Jr	287	Medinah, Ill.

(Graham won play-off 71 to 73)

1976	Jerry Pate	277	Al Geiberger	279	Atlanta Athletic
			Tom Weiskopf	279	Club, Duluth, Ga.
1977	Hubert Green	278	Lou Graham	279	Southern Hills,
					Okla.
1978	Andy North	285	Jesse Snead	286	Cherry Hills,
			Dave Stockton	286	Col.
1979	Hale Irwin	284	Jerry Pate	286	Inverness, Ohio
			Gary Player	286	
1980	Jack Nicklaus	272	Isao Aoki	274	Baltusrol, N.J.
1981	David Graham	273	George Burns	276	Merion, Pa.
			Bill Rogers	276	
1982	Tom Watson	282	Jack Nicklaus	284	Pebble Beach,
					Calif.
1983	Larry Nelson	280	Tom Watson	281	Oakmont, Pa.
1984	Fuzzy Zoeller	276	Greg Norman	276	Winged Foot,
					N.Y.

(Zoeller won play-off 67 to 75)

1985	Andy North	279	Dave Barr	280	Oakland Hills,
			T C Chen	280	Mich.
			Dennis Watson	280	
1986	Ray Floyd	279	Chip Beck	281	Shinnecock
			Lanny Wadkins	281	Hills, N.Y.

US MASTERS CHAMPIONSHIP

Played at the Augusta National Golf Course, Augusta, Georgia

Year	Winner	Score	Runner-up	Score
1934	Horton Smith	284	Craig Wood	285
1935	Gene Sarazen	282	Craig Wood	282

(Sarazen won play-off 144 to 149)

1936	Horton Smith	285	Harry Cooper	286
1937	Byron Nelson	283	Ralph Guldahl	285
1938	Henry Picard	285	Harry Cooper	287
			Ralph Guldahl	287
1939	Ralph Guldahl	279	Sam Snead	280
1940	Jimmy Demaret	280	Lloyd Mangrum	284
1941	Craig Wood	280	Byron Nelson	283
1942	Byron Nelson	280	Ben Hogan	280

(Nelson won play-off 69 to 70)

1943-45	No competition			
1946	Herman Keiser	282	Ben Hogan	283
1947	Jimmy Demaret	281	Byron Nelson	283
			Frank Stranahan	283
1948	Claude Harmon	279	Cary Middlecoff	284
1949	Sam Snead	282	Johnny Bulla	285
			Lloyd Mangrum	285
1950	Jimmy Demaret	283	Jim Ferrier	285
1951	Ben Hogan	280	Skee Riegel	282
1952	Sam Snead	286	Jack Burke Jr	290
1953	Ben Hogan	274	Porky Oliver Jr	279
1954	Sam Snead	289	Ben Hogan	289

(Snead won play-off 70 to 71)

1955	Cary Middlecoff	279	Ben Hogan	286
1956	Jack Burke Jr	289	Ken Venturi	290
1957	Doug Ford	283	Sam Snead	286
1958	Arnold Palmer	284	Doug Ford	285
			Fred Hawkins	285
1959	Art Wall Jr	284	Cary Middlecoff	285
1960	Arnold Palmer	282	Ken Venturi	283
1961	Gary Player	280	Arnold Palmer	281
			Charlie Coe	281
1962	Arnold Palmer	280	Gary Player	280
			Dow Finsterwald	280

(Palmer won play-off 68 to 71 to 77)

1963	Jack Nicklaus	286	Tony Lema	287
1964	Arnold Palmer	276	Dave Marr	282
			Jack Nicklaus	282
1965	Jack Nicklaus	271	Arnold Palmer	280
			Gary Player	280
1966	Jack Nicklaus	288	Tommy Jacobs	288
			Gay Brewer	288

(Nicklaus won play-off 70 to 72 to 78)

1967	Gay Brewer	280	Bobby Nichols	281
1968	Bob Goalby	277	Roberto de Vicenzo	278

US MASTERS CHAMPIONSHIP (contd)

Year	Winner	Score	Runner-up	Score
1969	George Archer	281	Billy Casper	282
			George Knudson	282
			Tom Weiskopf	282
1970	Billy Casper	279	Gene Littler	279
	(Casper won play-off 69 to 74)			
1971	Charles Coody	279	Johnny Miller	281
			Jack Nicklaus	281
1972	Jack Nicklaus	286	Bruce Crampton	289
			Bobby Mitchell	289
			Tom Weiskopf	289
1973	Tommy Aaron	283	Jesse Snead	284
1974	Gary Player	278	Dave Stockton	280
			Tom Weiskopf	280
1975	Jack Nicklaus	276	Johnny Miller	277
			Tom Weiskopf	277
1976	Ray Floyd	271	Ben Crenshaw	279
1977	Tom Watson	276	Jack Nicklaus	278
1978	Gary Player	277	Rod Funseth	278
			Hubert Green	278
			Tom Watson	278
1979	Fuzzy Zoeller	280	Ed Sneed	280
			Tom Watson	280
	(Zoeller won play-off at second extra hole)			
1980	Seve Ballesteros	275	Gibby Gilbert	279
			Jack Newton	279
1981	Tom Watson	280	Johnny Miller	282
			Jack Nicklaus	282
1982	Craig Stadler	284	Dan Pohl	284
	(Stadler won play-off at first extra hole)			
1983	Seve Ballesteros	280	Ben Crenshaw	284
			Tom Kite	284
1984	Ben Crenshaw	277	Tom Watson	279
1985	Bernhard Langer	282	Seve Ballesteros	284
			Ray Floyd	284
			Curtis Strange	284
1986	Jack Nicklaus	279	Tom Kite	280
			Greg Norman	280

US PGA CHAMPIONSHIP

Held by matchplay from 1916 to 1957

Year	Winner	Runner-up	Venue	By
1916	Jim Barnes	Jock Hutchison	Siwanoy, N.Y.	1 hole
1917-18	No competition			
1919	Jim Barnes	Fred McLeod	Engineers Club, N.Y.	6 and 5
1920	Jock Hutchison	Douglas Edgar	Flossmoor, Ill.	1 hole
1921	Walter Hagen	Jim Barnes	Inwood, N.Y.	3 and 2
1922	Gene Sarazen	Emmet French	Oakmont, Pa.	4 and 3
1923	Gene Sarazen	Walter Hagen	Pelham, N.Y.	38th hole
1924	Walter Hagen	Jim Barnes	French Lick, Ind.	2 holes
1925	Walter Hagen	Bill Mehlhorn	Olympic Fields, Ill.	6 and 4
1926	Walter Hagen	Leo Diegel	Salisbury, N.Y.	4 and 3
1927	Walter Hagen	Joe Turnesa	Cedar Crest, Tex.	1 hole
1928	Leo Diegel	Al Espinosa	Five Farms, Md.	6 and 5
1929	Leo Diegel	John Farrell	Hillcrest, Calif.	6 and 4
1930	Tommy Armour	Gene Sarazen	Fresh Meadow, N.Y.	1 hole
1931	Tom Creavy	Densmore Shute	Wannamoisett, R.I.	2 and 1
1932	Olin Dutra	Frank Walsh	Keller, Minn.	4 and 3
1933	Gene Sarazen	Willie Goggin	Blue Mound, Wis.	5 and 4
1934	Paul Runyan	Craig Wood	Park, N.Y.	38th hole
1935	Johnny Revolta	Tommy Armour	Twin Hills, Okla.	5 and 4
1936	Densmore Shute	Jimmy Thomson	Pinehurst, N.C.	3 and 2
1937	Densmore Shute	Harold McSpaden	Pittsburgh, Pa.	37th hole
1938	Paul Runyan	Sam Snead	Shawnee, Pa.	8 and 7
1939	Henry Picard	Byron Nelson	Pomonok, N.Y.	37th hole
1940	Byron Nelson	Sam Snead	Hershey, Pa.	1 hole
1941	Vic Ghezzi	Byron Nelson	Cherry Hills, Col.	38th hole
1942	Sam Snead	Jim Turnesa	Seaview, N.J.	2 and 1
1943	No competition			
1944	Bob Hamilton	Byron Nelson	Manito, Wash.	1 hole
1945	Byron Nelson	Sam Byrd	Morraine, Ohio	4 and 3

Year	Winner	Runner-up	Venue	By
1946	Ben Hogan	Porky Oliver	Portland, Oreg.	6 and 4
1947	Jim Ferrier	Chick Harbert	Plum Hollow, Mich.	2 and 1
1948	Ben Hogan	Mike Turnesa	Norwood Hills, Mo.	7 and 6
1949	Sam Snead	Johnny Palmer	Hermitage, Va.	3 and 2
1950	Chandler Harper	Henry Williams	Scioto, Ohio	4 and 3
1951	Sam Snead	Walter Burkemo	Oakmont, Pa.	7 and 6
1952	Jim Turnesa	Chick Harbert	Big Spring, Ken.	1 hole
1953	Walter Burkemo	Felice Torza	Birmingham, Mich.	2 and 1
1954	Chick Harbert	Walter Burkemo	Keller, Minn.	4 and 3
1955	Doug Ford	Cary Middlecoff	Meadowbrook, Mich.	4 and 3
1956	Jack Burke	Ted Kroll	Blue Hill, Mass.	3 and 2
1957	Lionel Hebert	Dow Finsterwald	Miami Valley, Ohio	3 and 1

Changed to strokeplay

Year	Winner	Score	Runner-up	Score	Venue
1958	Dow Finsterwald	276	Billy Casper	278	Llanerch, Pa.
1959	Bob Rosburg	277	Jerry Barber	278	Minneapolis,
			Doug Sanders	278	Minn.
1960	Jay Hebert	281	Jim Ferrier	282	Firestone, Ohio
1961	Jerry Barber	277	Don January	277	Olympia Fields, Ill.
	(Barber won play-off 67 to 68)				
1962	Gary Player	278	Bob Goalby	279	Aronimink, Pa.
1963	Jack Nicklaus	279	Dave Ragan	281	Dallas Athletic, Tex.
1964	Bobby Nichols	271	Jack Nicklaus	274	Columbus,
			Arnold Palmer	274	Ohio
1965	Dave Marr	280	Billy Casper	282	Laurel Valley, Pa.
			Jack Nicklaus	282	
1966	Al Geiberger	280	Dudley Wysong	284	Firestone, Ohio
1967	Don January	281	Don Massengale	281	Columbine, Col.
	(January won play-off 69 to 71)				
1968	Julius Boros	281	Bob Charles	282	Pecan Valley, Tex.
			Arnold Palmer	282	
1969	Ray Floyd	276	Gary Player	277	NCR Club, Dayton, Ohio
1970	Dave Stockton	279	Bob Murphy	281	Southern Hills, Oklahoma
1971	Jack Nicklaus	281	Billy Casper	283	PGA National, Fla.
1972	Gary Player	281	Tommy Aaron	283	Oakland Hills,
			Jim Jamieson	283	Mich.
1973	Jack Nicklaus	277	Bruce Crampton	281	Canterbury, Ohio
1974	Lee Trevino	276	Jack Nicklaus	277	Tanglewood, N.C.
1975	Jack Nicklaus	276	Bruce Crampton	278	Firestone, Akron, Ohio
1976	Dave Stockton	281	Ray Floyd	282	Congressional,
			Don January	282	Md.
1977	Lanny Wadkins	282	Gene Littler	282	Pebble Beach, Calif.
	(Wadkins won sudden-death play-off at the third hole)				
1978	John Mahaffey	276	Jerry Pate	276	Oakmont, Pa.
			Tom Watson	276	
	(Mahaffey won sudden-death play-off at second hole)				
1979	David Graham	272	Ben Crenshaw	272	Oakland Hills,
	(Graham won sudden-death play-off at third hole)			Mich.
1980	Jack Nicklaus	274	Andy Bean	281	Oak Hill, N.Y.
1981	Larry Nelson	273	Fuzzy Zoeller	277	Atlanta Athletic Club, Duluth, Ga.
1982	Ray Floyd	272	Lanny Wadkins	275	Southern Hills, Okla.
1983	Hal Sutton	274	Jack Nicklaus	275	Riviera, Calif.
1984	Lee Trevino	273	Gary Player	277	Shoal Creek, Ala.
			Lanny Wadkins	277	
1985	Hubert Green	278	Lee Trevino	280	Cherry Hills, Col.
1986	Bob Tway	276	Greg Norman	278	Inverness, Ohio

WORLD MATCH-PLAY CHAMPIONSHIP

Played at Wentworth, Surrey

Sponsored by Piccadilly until 1976, by Colgate in 1977 and 1978, and by Suntory from 1979

Year	Winner	Runner-up	By
1964	Arnold Palmer	Neil Coles	2 and 1
1965	Gary Player	Peter Thomson	3 and 2
1966	Gary Player	Jack Nicklaus	6 and 4
1967	Arnold Palmer	Peter Thomson	1 hole
1968	Gary Player	Bob Charles	1 hole
1969	Bob Charles	Gene Littler	37th hole
1970	Jack Nicklaus	Lee Trevino	2 and 1
1971	Gary Player	Jack Nicklaus	5 and 4
1972	Tom Weiskopf	Lee Trevino	4 and 3
1973	Gary Player	Graham Marsh	40th hole
1974	Hale Irwin	Gary Player	3 and 1
1975	Hale Irwin	Al Geiberger	4 and 2
1976	David Graham	Hale Irwin	38th hole
1977	Graham Marsh	Ray Floyd	5 and 3
1978	Isao Aoki	Simon Owen	3 and 2
1979	Bill Rogers	Isao Aoki	1 hole
1980	Greg Norman	Sandy Lyle	1 hole
1981	Seve Ballesteros	Ben Crenshaw	1 hole
1982	Seve Ballesteros	Sandy Lyle	37th hole
1983	Greg Norman	Nick Faldo	3 and 2
1984	Seve Ballesteros	Bernhard Langer	2 and 1
1985	Seve Ballesteros	Bernhard Langer	6 and 5

RYDER CUP

Year	Winners	USA Total	Great Britain and Ireland Total	Captains USA	Britain	Venue
1927	USA	9½	2½	Walter Hagen	Ted Ray	Worcester, Mass.
1929	Britain	5	7	Walter Hagen	George Duncan	Moortown
1931	USA	9	3	Walter Hagen	Charles Whitcombe	Scioto, Ohio
1933	Britain	5½	6½	Walter Hagen	J H Taylor*	Southport and Ainsdale
1935	USA	9	3	Walter Hagen	Charles Whitcombe	Ridgewood, N.J.
1937	USA	8	4	Walter Hagen*	Charles Whitcombe	Southport and Ainsdale
1947	USA	11	1	Ben Hogan	Henry Cotton	Portland, Oreg.
1949	USA	7	5	Ben Hogan*	Charles Whitcombe*	Ganton, Scarborough
1951	USA	9½	2½	Sam Snead	Arthur Lacey*	Pinehurst, N.C.
1953	USA	6½	5½	Lloyd Mangrum	Henry Cotton*	Wentworth
1955	USA	8	4	Chick Harbert	Dai Rees	Palm Springs, Calif.
1957	Britain	4½	7½	Jack Burke	Dai Rees	Lindrick
1959	USA	8½	3½	Sam Snead	Dai Rees	Palm Desert, Calif.
1961	USA	14½	9½	Jerry Barber	Dai Rees	Royal Lytham
1963	USA	23	9	Arnold Palmer	Johnny Fallon*	Atlanta, Ga.
1965	USA	19½	12½	Byron Nelson*	Harry Weetman*	Royal Birkdale
1967	USA	23½	8½	Ben Hogan*	Dai Rees*	Houston, Tex.
1969	(tie)	16	16	Sam Snead*	Eric Brown*	Royal Birkdale
1971	USA	18½	13½	Jay Hebert*	Eric Brown*	St Louis, Mo.
1973	USA	19	13	Jack Burke*	Bernard Hunt*	Muirfield
1975	USA	21	11	Arnold Palmer*	Bernard Hunt*	Laurel Valley, Pa.
1977	USA	12½	7½	Dow Finsterwald*	Brian Huggett*	Royal Lytham

In 1979, players from continental Europe were invited to join the Great Britain and Ireland team.

*Non-playing captain

Year	Winners	USA Total	Europe Total	Captains USA	Europe	Venue
1979	USA	17	11	Billy Casper*	John Jacobs*	Greenbrier, W.Va.
1981	USA	18½	9½	Dave Marr*	John Jacobs	Walton Heath
1983	USA	14½	13½	Jack Nicklaus*	Tony Jacklin*	PGA National, Fla.
1985	Europe	11½	16½	Lee Trevino*	Tony Jacklin*	The Belfry

WALKER CUP

Year	Winners	USA Total	Great Britain and Ireland Total	Captains USA	Britain	Venue
1922	USA	8	4	William Fownes Jr	Robert Harris	National Links, N.Y.
1923	USA	6½	5½	Robert Gardner	Robert Harris	St Andrews
1924	USA	9	3	Robert Gardner	Cyril Tolley	Garden City, N.Y.
1926	USA	6½	5½	Robert Gardner	Robert Harris	St Andrews
1928	USA	11	1	Bobby Jones	Dr William Tweddell	Chicago GC, Wheaton, Ill.
1930	USA	10	2	Bobby Jones	Roger Wethered	Royal St George's
1932	USA	9½	2½	Francis Ouimet	Tony Torrance	Brookline, Mass.
1934	USA	9½	2½	Francis Ouimet	Hon Michael Scott	St Andrews
1936	USA	10½	1½	Francis Ouimet*	Dr William Tweddell	Pine Valley, N.J.
1938	GB&I	4½	7½	Francis Ouimet*	John Beck	St Andrews
1947	USA	8	4	Francis Ouimet*	John Beck	St Andrews
1949	USA	10	2	Francis Ouimet*	Percy 'Laddie' Lucas	Winged Foot, N.Y.
1951	USA	7½	4½	William Turnesa*	Raymond Oppenheimer	Royal Birkdale
1953	USA	9	3	Charles Yates*	Lt-Col Tony Duncan	Kittansett Club, Mass.
1955	USA	10	2	William Campbell*	G Alec Hill*	St Andrews
1957	USA	8½	3½	Charles Coe*	Gerald Micklem*	Minikhada Club, Minn.
1959	USA	9	3	Charles Coe	Gerald Micklem*	Muirfield
1961	USA	11	1	Jack Westland*	Charles Lawrie*	Seattle, Wash.
1963	USA	14	10	Richard Tufts*	Charles Lawrie*	Ailsa Course, Turnberry
1965	(tie)	12	12	John Fischer*	Joe Carr*	Baltimore, Md.
1967	USA	15	9	Jess Sweetser*	Joe Carr	Royal St George's
1969	USA	13	11	Billy Joe Patton*	Michael Bonallack	Milwaukee, Wis.
1971	GB&I	11	13	John Winters Jr*	Michael Bonallack	St Andrews
1973	USA	14	10	Jess Sweetser*	Dr David Marsh	Brookline, Mass.
1975	USA	15½	8½	Dr Ed Updegraff*	Dr David Marsh*	St Andrews
1977	USA	16	8	Lou Oehmig*	Sandy Saddler*	Shinnecock Hills, N.Y.
1979	USA	15½	8½	Richard Siderowf*	Rodney Foster*	Muirfield
1981	USA	15	9	Jim Gabrielsen*	Rodney Foster*	Cypress Point, Calif.
1983	USA	13½	10½	Jay Sigel	Charlie Green*	Hoylake
1985	USA	13	11	Jay Sigel	Charlie Green*	Pine Valley, N.J.

*Non-playing captain

GLOSSARY

Ace A hole made in one stroke, i.e. a hole in one.

Address Taking a stance from which to hit the ball.

Albatross The term for a score of three under par at one hole.

Approach The shot that is played when a player is sufficiently close to reach the green with that shot.

Apron The grass area immediately bordering the putting green; it is generally mowed lower than the fairway.

Baff To strike the ball with the sole of the club-head and so send the ball into the air.

Baffy The term for a wooden club used to hit lofted shots.

Banana shot A very badly sliced shot sending the ball violently from left to right through the air.

Birdie The term applied for a score of one under par at one hole.

Blind hole One where the green cannot be seen by the player when executing his approach slot.

Bogey In strict terms the number of strokes which an average player should take at a hole. In America this term refers to a score of one over par at one specific hole and in Britain it is nowadays used with the same meaning.

Brassy An original term for a wooden club with a brass sole plate. It is regarded today as a 2-wood.

Break A reference to the percentage of turn there might be in a specific putt.

Bulger An original term for a wooden club with a convex face.

Bye The holes that remain after a match between players has been concluded.

Caddie A person who carries the golfer's clubs.

Carry The distance from where the ball is struck to where it lands. Sometimes the term is used to pinpoint a particular place which must be reached from the tee if the player is to be in the best of positions.

Casual water Snow, ice and any temporary accumulation of water from where a player can pick up and drop his ball without incurring a penalty.

Chip A shot made close to the green – usually from out of the rough encircling the green.

Chip and run A shot purposely hit low so that it lands on the green then rolls towards the flag.

Cleek An original term for an iron-headed club used for driving and sometimes for putting.

Cross-bunker A reference to a bunker that is in a fairway area so that it requires a player to hit over it on the way from the tee to the green.

Dead A ball is said to be dead when it lies so near the hole that the putt is an absolute certainty.

Divot A piece of turf sliced out of the fairway which should be immediately replaced by the player.

Dormy A player is said to be 'dormy' when he is ahead by the number of holes which remain in a match.

Draw To make the ball move from right to left through the air.

Driver The club employed for striking the first shot at par four or par five holes. The wooden head is larger than the head of any other club in the bag and the angle of loft is usually less than 12 degrees.

Eagle The term applied for a score of two under the specified par at one hole.

Fade To make the ball move from left to right through the air.

Fairway That part of a hole which is usually mown short so that it forms a 'channel' from the tee to the green.

Flag-stick Placed in the hole so that a player can see where the cup has been cut on a specific green.

Fog Moss or rank grass.

Fore A warning cry to anybody in range of a shot.

Fourball Four players, in teams of two, each playing their own ball.

Foursome A match in which two golfers play on each side. Each pair of players share a ball, hitting alternate shots at any given hole and alternating hole by hole when teeing off.

Fried egg A slang expression for a ball that is buried in a bunker.

Fringe See Apron.

Gallery The spectators watching a tournament.

Get up and down To pitch or chip then one-putt.

Gobble An original term for a well struck, hard putt which, had it not gone into the hole, would have gone some distance beyond.

Grain The way that the grass lies on a green, as with cat's fur.

Grand Slam In modern terms the four championships of the world which are the US Masters, US Open, British Open and US PGA Championship.

Green The putting surface for each individual hole.

Green fee The amount that one pays to play a course.

Grip The term used for the way in which a club is held in preparation for hitting the ball. Also that part of the handle of a club which is gripped.

Gutty A slang term for the original ball made of gutta-percha which is a rubbery substance obtained from the sap of certain Malayan trees.

Half or halved A hole is declared

to be halved when each side takes the same number of shots. A halved match is drawn.

Handicap The method by which any two players can be equally matched in spite of one being better than the other. A player is handicapped by regularly submitting completed scorecards to the club where he is a member.

Hanging lie A ball that is on a downward slope so that the player has to over-stretch to play the intended shot.

Hazard A general term for bunker, long grass, road, water, whin, molehill or other bad ground, although in today's golfing vocabulary it usually refers to a bunker, ditch or pond.

Head to head A term used for one player taking on another in an individual match.

Heel The part of the club-head nearest the hosel.

Honour The right to play off first from a tee, usually earned by a player scoring less than his opponent at the previous hole.

Hook An exaggerated draw – in other words a ball which moves further in the air from right to left than intended by the player.

Hosel The socket in a club into which the shaft fits.

Iron A club made of the material which the name implies, with the head more or less laid back to loft the ball. From the number one club to the wedge the iron face becomes larger and more lofted.

Lag To roll up a putt to a certain holing distance.

Lateral water hazard A natural pond or ditch that runs parallel to the fairway and from where there is a specific procedure within the rules for taking relief.

Level (or like) as we lie When both sides, or both players, have played the same number of strokes.

Lie The situation of the ball on the turf, i.e. a good or a bad lie.

Links The open downs or heath on which golf is played. Nowadays it usually refers to a seaside course since this is laid out on land referred to as linksland.

Loft To hit the ball so that it arcs through the air; also used for the angle of a club's face by which to achieve this.

Long iron In modern parlance this usually relates to an iron club of number one, two, three or four.

Mashie, mashy An original term

for a straight-faced, iron-headed club which would be equivalent to a modern 5-iron.

Match play Reckoning the score by holes.

Medal play See Stroke play.

Nap See Grain.

Niblick An original term for a small, narrow-headed, heavy iron club used when in a bad lie.

Nineteenth The clubhouse bar.

Out of bounds When the ball is struck beyond a boundary which designates the limit of the course.

Par The theoretical score that a professional is expected to make at a specific hole.

PGA The Professional Golfers' Association.

PGA European Tour The body that organizes the professional tour in Europe.

Pin See Flag-stick.

Pitch A lofted shot usually executed from out of the rough surrounding a green.

Pitching wedge The implement used for playing a pitch shot.

Play club An original term for a wooden-headed club with a full-length shaft, more or less supple, with which the ball could be driven to the greatest distance. In modern terms, a driver.

Postage stamp A small green.

Preferred lie Under local rules this will permit a player to improve his lie when on the fairway without incurring a penalty stroke.

Punch shot To slam the club down into the ball with a short swing so that it keeps the ball low into a wind.

Putter The implement used for strokes on the putting surface.

Reload A golfer's expression for taking another ball after hitting the first attempt out of bounds.

Rough Areas adjacent to the fairways which are in their natural state, i.e. not mowed.

Royal and Ancient The governing body of the game based in St Andrews, Scotland.

Rub of the green A favourable or unfavourable happening for which there is no redress.

Sand iron, sand wedge A club with a sharply-angled face, usually employed for hitting the ball out of a bunker.

Scratch player One who receives no allowance in a handicap.

Set A full complement of clubs. A player today may, under the rules, put a maximum of 14 clubs in his bag.

Shaft The stick or handle of a club.

Short game A reference to that part of the game played on or around the putting surface.

Short iron A term usually applied to an eight, nine or ten club. A ten is a pitching wedge.

Slice To hit the ball so that it moves violently from left to right through the air.

Snap-hook A shot that curves violently from right to left through the air.

Sole The flat bottom of the club head.

Spoon An original term for a wooden-headed club with a lofted head so that it would loft the ball.

Square When a game stands evenly balanced, i.e. neither side being ahead.

Stableford A method of scoring in which a player is awarded one point for a score of one over par at a specific hole; two points for a par; three points for a birdie; four points for an eagle, etc.

Stroke holes The hole or holes at which, in handicapping, a stroke is given by the better player to the inferior player.

Stroke play Reckoning the score by strokes.

Stymie An original term, no longer applicable, for when a player's ball lies in the line of that of an opponent.

Swale A small hump.

Sweet spot Centre of mass of the club-head, hence the point of the club-face which must contact the ball for optimum effect.

Swing The sweep of a club in hitting the ball.

Tee Originally a pat of sand on which the ball was placed for the first stroke at each hole. Nowadays a tee is made of wood or plastic.

Tee marker The designated spot on a teeing ground on a given day for starting the playing of a hole.

Teeing ground An area specifically cared for so that it offers a player the chance to take a good stance for the first shot at each hole.

Teeing up The act of placing the ball on a tee to strike the first shot at any given hole.

Texas wedge A reference to a putter when it is employed for hitting a shot from off the green or from out of a bunker.

Top To hit a ball above its centre.

Twitch See Yips.

Underclub To take one, two or more clubs less than that required to enable the ball to reach the desired target.

Wedge A sharply angled club usually referred to as a pitching wedge or a sand wedge and employed for extracting the ball from a difficult or hazardous lie.

Whin Furze or gorse.

Whipping The pitched twine uniting the head of the club to the handle.

Wood A club with a head made of wood such as persimmon.

Yips Uncontrollable action on a putter which causes a player to consistently miss short putts.

INDEX